ARKANSAS CIVIL WAR HERITAGE

A LEGACY OF HONOR

W. STUART TOWNS

THE
History
PRESS

Published by The History Press
Charleston, SC 29403
www.historypress.net

Front cover, top: The Thirty-fourth Volunteer Infantry, Company K, at the Confederate reunion in Prairie Grove, Washington County, 1900s. Birch E. Grabill, Fayetteville, photography. *Courtesy Shiloh Museum of Ozark History/An Web Collection (s-2013-35)*. *Back cover, inset*: Brochure for the 1892 Phillips County Confederate Veterans reunion. *Courtesy Old State House Museum Collection*.

First published 2013

Manufactured in the United States

ISBN 978.1.62619.192.1

Library of Congress CIP data applied for.

Notice: The information in this book is true and complete to the best of our knowledge. It is offered without guarantee on the part of the author or The History Press. The author and The History Press disclaim all liability in connection with the use of this book.

I dedicate this book to the late Dr. Ralph T. Eubanks, who reinforced my love of the South and of Arkansas during my many classes with him in Old Main at the University of Arkansas and throughout my career. Ralph was the epitome of the southern scholar and gentleman and a great influence on my life.

CONTENTS

ACKNOWLEDGEMENTS

Writing a book, even a labor of love like this one, requires the help of many people: librarians, fellow researchers in the subject, archivists, curators, friends and relatives. *Arkansas Civil War Heritage* was no exception. At the risk of leaving out someone who helped tremendously, I want to thank the following: Liz Robbins at the Garland County Historical Society; Wendy Richter and Ray Granade at the Ouachita Baptist University Library; Bill Leach of the White County Historical Society; Angela Gibbs, curator at the Jacksonport State Park; Betty Luck, research librarian at the United Daughters of the Confederacy Headquarters in Richmond, Virginia; Martha Koon and Judy Coleman of the UDC in Hot Springs; Pamela Trammell of the Texas-Arkansas-Louisiana UDC Research Center in Texarkana, Texas; Toinette Madison, director of the Boone County Heritage Museum; Paula Barnett, publisher of the Woodruff County *Monitor* in McCrory; Ron Kelley of the Delta Cultural Center in Helena; Dr. Bill J. Gurley; Joellen Maack of the Old State House Museum; the staff of the Marianna/Lee County Museum; Peggy Lloyd and Gail Martin at the Southwest Arkansas Archives in Washington, Arkansas; Betty Kellum, Drew County Archives and Historical Society; Judy Fava, director, Lake Village, Arkansas Public Library; the staff at the Arkansas History Commission; Richard Davies, director of the Arkansas Department of Parks and Tourism and members of his staff; John Coski of the Museum of the Confederacy in Richmond; Charlie Crafford of Cotton Plant; Pat Rowbotham, Lance Spanke and Mark Rogers of the Johnson County Historical Society and Heritage Museum;

Guice Howell of Clarksville; Sherryl Miller, Lonoke County Museum; Marie Demeroukas, Shiloh Museum of Ozark History, Springdale; Dean DeBolt, University of West Florida Library; Ellen Carain, Newport Public Library; Charity Park, Pope County Library; Alice Gatewood, Helena–West Helena Public Library; and Kaye Lundgren, University of Arkansas Little Rock Center for Arkansas History & Culture. I am sure there are others whom I am overlooking; forgive me.

The most helpful and supportive cast member was my wife, Helen Ruth, with whom I celebrated our fiftieth wedding anniversary at the peak of the research and writing stress of this project; thank you, Helen Ruth, for hanging in there for all those years and especially these long months of travel to libraries and Civil War sites across the great state of Arkansas.

INTRODUCTION

Why, you ask, another book on the Civil War? Unbelievably, there are still topics to be explored that will tell us more about this most memorable event of our history. *Arkansas Civil War Heritage* is not about the war itself, but it helps explain why the public memory of that contest is still alive and well in the twenty-first century. I hope it will also inspire you to learn more about our Civil War history and heritage in our state and across the South and that that will, in turn, help you become more aware and concerned about protecting and preserving this history, tradition and heritage. We must all realize that Civil War history belongs to all Americans, whether we are white or black, and that we cannot change or erase our history.

Since my days as an undergraduate at the University of Arkansas studying the history of southern rhetoric and oratory, I have been fascinated by the lasting effect of the Civil War on southern culture. Part of that narrative is the story of the commemoration of Confederate Memorial Day across the South, the erecting and dedication of hundreds of monuments to the Confederacy and the reunions held for years by the veterans of that bloody conflict. The sesquicentennial of the Civil War is being observed with countless reenactments of battles and skirmishes, educational programs and lectures, books and videos and myriad other educational and entertaining events. Why is the Civil War still so important to Arkansans, southerners and, indeed, all Americans a century and a half after General Robert E. Lee rode away from Appomattox? *Arkansas Civil War Heritage* answers that question by describing the postwar story as it evolved across the Natural State.

Several books on Civil War Confederate memory focus on the Confederate monuments of a specific state, and there are some fine examples of these.[1] *Arkansas Civil War Heritage* expands that perspective of memorial gratitude to dead heroes of the war to include a narrative about how Arkansans celebrated Confederate Memorial Day and also honored the living soldiers and sailors with organized reunions of the old veterans. Finally, we take a look at the ongoing commemoration of the heritage of the Civil War in contemporary, twenty-first-century events such as living history demonstrations, modern museum exhibits, battle reenactments, continued celebrations of Confederate Memorial Day and the contemporary work of heritage groups, such as the Sons of Confederate Veterans, the United Daughters of the Confederacy and the Military Order of Stars and Bars across the Natural State.

The South was not only determined to follow the time-honored conventions of memorializing the dead as communities have done throughout history, but it also faced other issues that required resolution. It was defeated in a war it fully expected to win. The death toll was at an unprecedented level as hundreds of thousands of men failed to return home (and many of those who did were maimed for life). Many thousands were buried far from home in unmarked and unknown graves as the modern military approach to deal with the dead was yet undeveloped.

In order to appropriately and fully honor the dead, southerners created Confederate Memorial Day or Decoration Day, as it was called in some places. They soon began to erect stone and bronze monuments and organized reunions so the old soldiers could rejoin their comrades in recalling memories of their war experiences and learn to cope better with the changed and changing new environment in the region. Chapter one provides the regional context for this effort to create the public narrative and memory of the war. Understanding the regionwide movement to honor and memorialize the dead will give the reader a broader context within which to fit the Arkansas campaign to create and sustain the public narrative of the Civil War.

This public memory was created in many ways, but the regionwide commemoration of Confederate Memorial Day, founded and sustained by women of the defeated Confederacy through their local memorial associations, was perhaps the most significant. Chapter two discusses some examples of Confederate Memorial Day in Arkansas.

Soon, women of the South began to campaign to raise countless monuments to Confederate heroes and leaders, the women who remained back home and the common soldiers of the Confederacy. By 1914, communities throughout the South had erected over one thousand monuments to honor the Confederate dead and the Southern cause. Out of the many local ladies' memorial associations and ladies' monument associations grew the United Daughters of the Confederacy (UDC), which was organized in 1894. There are over fifty monuments in Arkansas, and chapter three will examine the monument movement across the state.

Finally, as the war-torn veterans recovered from much of the horror of war and the bitter sting of defeat, they began to meet with their old buddies in their local units. Dozens of local veterans' groups were founded. In 1889, the United Confederate Veterans (UCV) organization was established, and its annual reunions drew thousands of old soldiers and their families to various locations around the South. Two years later, the Sons of Confederate Veterans (SCV) was formed, and it is still in operation today, as is the UDC. Chapter four describes some of these reunions as they occurred in Arkansas.

For decades, thousands of parades, speeches and public celebrations of one kind or another were devoted to honoring the Confederacy. The power of that rhetoric and oratory of the Lost Cause is demonstrated in the persistence of the mind-set that was developed and retained by many white southerners throughout the twentieth century and on into the twenty-first century. The goals of the oratory at these events were to defend the South, explain the crushing defeat and lift up the spirits of southerners by praising their heroes and celebrating their families' contributions to the Southern cause. They were successful as evidenced today by the current sesquicentennial events being held across the South and the nation. The pervasive and prevailing narrative that was fashioned out of all this effort formed a foundation out of which generations of white southerners have shaped and lived their lives.

In some form or another, these events are still being commemorated as we go through the sesquicentennial of the "the Waw" as Mark Twain described it in his *Life on the Mississippi* when he wrote:

> [In the South,] *every man you meet was in the war; and every lady you meet saw the war. The war is the chief topic of conversation. The interest in it is vivid and constant; the interest in other topics is fleeting. Mention of the war will wake up a dull company and set their tongues going, when nearly any other topic would fail. In the South, the war is what A.D. is elsewhere; they date from it. All day long you hear things "placed" as having happened since the waw; or du'in the waw; or befo' the waw; or right aftah the waw; or 'bout two yeahs or five yeahs, or ten yeahs befo' the waw or aftah the waw. It shows how intimately every individual was visited, in his own person, by that tremendous episode.*[2]

The three events we explore here help explain how the South and Arkansas built and maintained the public memory of that "tremendous episode" and its effects even in the twenty-first century.

While not in the South, it would be an oversight to fail to mention a major project occurring in 2013 as an example of the continuing heritage of the Civil War: returning the location of the pivotal event of the Civil War—Gettysburg National Military Park—to its 1863 appearance. The National Park Service, with the help of private organizations and foundations, has been working since 1999 to restore the battlefield to the way it was seen by Union and Confederate troops in early July 1863. Among other projects, such as removing the cyclorama building and replacing the old visitor center with a modern version, it is clearing trees in various locations so visitors can see what the soldiers saw and better understand how the landscape and terrain affected the battle. In some places, it has planted trees to match what was in place 150 years ago. For example, the peach orchard, through which Confederate troops advanced during the battle, has been replanted. The project is continuing with a $7 to $8 million rehabilitation of the Little Round Top area, and other projects are still being planned.[3]

Debates continue over the public use of Confederate memorabilia such as the battle flag or the singing of "Dixie" in a public location. Confederate Memorial Day is still observed in the region and in Arkansas; it is an official state-sanctioned event on the Saturday before Easter each year on the grounds of the state capitol building. Monuments are still being erected, maintained and refurbished as the years take their toll on the stone or bronze. Roadside markers and interpretive panels are being added to the sites of battles and skirmishes, camps, hospitals and other sites related to the war.

Perhaps most important, many organizations are still actively meeting and carrying on the tradition of the veterans' reunions. The old veterans are long gone, but the Sons of Confederate Veterans is viable and highly visible, as its camps dot the South. The United Daughters of the Confederacy still encourages educating the young in the history of the Civil War and the Confederacy and sponsors scholarships and educational events for the community. The Children of the Confederacy organization continues to introduce youth to the history of the Confederacy and the South. More contemporary organizations such the Civil War Round Table and the Military Order of the Stars and Bars (similar to the SCV, but the ancestor must have been a Confederate army or navy officer) are flourishing around the region.

A few examples out of many from across the South and Arkansas illustrate the staying power of the heritage and tradition of the Civil War from both sides of the debate. Monuments are being built and dedicated to Southern Civil War heroes. On May 26, 1997, a new Confederate monument was raised and dedicated in Smithfield, Tennessee. In 2001, plans were announced for a new memorial to be built in Newton, North Carolina, and it was dedicated in 2005. Sanford, North Carolina, dedicated a memorial to Robert E. Lee on Lee's birthday in 2008. As recently as the summer of 2011, a new monument was erected in Mount Hebron Cemetery in Winchester, Virginia, to memorialize twenty Arkansas Confederates killed at Greenbrier River near Winchester. In March 2012, the Civil War Trust announced a $1.3 million fundraising campaign to preserve two parcels of land near the Cedar Creek and Belle Grove National Historical Park in the Shenandoah Valley, about eighty miles from Washington, D.C. The Museum of the Confederacy, headquartered in Richmond, Virginia, opened a $7.5 million site at Appomattox on March 31, 2013. The new facility, located at the junction of U.S. 460 and SR 24, is one of three projected sites for the Museum of the Confederacy. The other two are planned for Fredericksburg and Hampton Roads, Virginia, in the coming years.

Other recent events point to the debates over the use of Confederate memorabilia that are still raging across the South between those who use the flag and other symbols of the Confederacy to honor their heritage and those for whom they bring back the memory of slavery and racism. In September 2011, the City of Lexington, Virginia, home of Washington and Lee University, passed a city ordinance that allows only the city, state and U.S. flags to fly from city light poles. The SCV protested the ruling and filed a suit against the city. Resident David Compton said the flag represents "slavery and it still represents slavery and it will always represent slavery, and it's disgraceful to continue to fly it like this." Longtime SCV member Dan Boyette reminded the city residents that "we're tired of everyone putting down our symbols and our heritage, and we're going to stand up and fight. I'm passionate about this because this is my family, this is my blood, this is my heritage." On the annual Lee/Jackson Day celebration in January 2012, members of the Sons of Confederate Veterans stood under downtown light poles, holding Confederate flags. The commentary about the event said, "They came for love of God, Country and the privilege of honoring America's diversified history and inheritance."[4]

In November 2011, the Texas Department of Motor Vehicles Board voted unanimously to reject a proposal for a specialty license plate featuring the Confederate flag. They made this decision after hearing hours of testimony opposing the plates.[5]

On November 17, 2012, the Old State House Museum in Little Rock sponsored an 1862 Civil War Living History event regarding the political and military buildup to the Prairie Grove Campaign and Battle in the northwest corner of the state.[6]

In 2012, the City of Helena–West Helena, Arkansas, dedicated a rebuilt Union fort, Fort Curtis, in the downtown area and has created an automobile tour of the city and surrounding area that highlights and identifies the many Civil War sites in Phillips County. The city also dedicated in 2013 an area known as Freedom Park, which remembers and honors the thousands of slaves, called contraband, who followed General Curtis's troops into Helena after the Union forces took the city and who were freed, cared for and provided a new place to call home. Unfortunately, their numbers overwhelmed the ability of the military to adequately care for them, and many died during their stay in Helena. Many of the males joined the U.S. Army Colored Troops at Fort Curtis, and their service is explained through narrative panels at Freedom Park.

Throughout the sesquicentennial years, the Arkansas Civil War Sesquicentennial Commission has been strongly supporting a statewide, all-inclusive celebration of the heritage of the war. A magnificent traveling exhibit titled "Fought in Earnest: Civil War Arkansas" has been making its rounds of sites such as libraries, college campuses, museums and other venues. In addition, many markers have been approved and installed at Civil War battle sites and other locations relevant to the war years. A Civil War highway trail has been identified and clearly marked with "Civil War Trail" signs throughout the state. A Civil War Passport Program has been implemented so that travelers around the state can be encouraged to see as many of the Civil War sites as possible. Chapter five explores in further detail what Arkansas is doing during the sesquicentennial to continue the commemoration of the Civil War and to expand our knowledge of this most epic event in our nation's history.

I hope this book will encourage you to visit the sites discussed here, study the events that challenged our nation as it had never been challenged before or since and learn about the people who hope to preserve the memory and the heritage of who we are as southerners and as Americans. The Civil War touched the lives of every American in 1861–65, and I encourage you to work to understand it and share your understanding with others. We cannot turn our backs on our history, our family heritage or our state, region or nation's history. The Civil War touched all Americans—it is part of who we are. Seeing and learning about these monuments, memorial days and reunions can help us all understand this momentous event that transformed our nation a century and a half ago.

1

CREATING AND SUSTAINING THE HERITAGE OF THE CIVIL WAR ACROSS THE SOUTH

THE BIG PICTURE

The Civil War is still alive and well throughout the South and Arkansas. Before we get into a detailed examination of the phenomenon in Arkansas, we will briefly look at these three events as they developed across the South in the last decades of the nineteenth century and on into the twentieth century. All three played roles in helping white southerners come to grips with total defeat and absolute devastation. A wide, regional perspective will give us the big picture of what was happening across the defeated Confederate States of America and help us better understand how the public memory of the Civil War was created and sustained.

CONFEDERATE MEMORIAL OR DECORATION DAY

Never before had the nation faced the enormity of the Civil War's death statistics. Over 620,000 soldiers, Northern and Southern, died during 1861–65. This figure is about equal to the total number of American troops and sailors who died in all the nation's other wars prior to Vietnam (the Revolutionary War, War of 1812, Mexican War, Spanish-American War, World War I, World War II and Korea). One out of five white Southern men of military age did not survive the war; many died in battle, but twice as many others died of their wounds or disease in an era that had not developed adequate sanitation practices or vaccines.

Even before the Civil War ground to an end in the spring of 1865, Southern women began to care for the graves of Confederate soldiers. This grassroots movement began to gain momentum and organization in 1866, when Mrs. Mary Williams of Columbus, Georgia, took a leadership role in promoting April 26 as a regionwide day of observance in memory of those who had died in the war. As time passed, Decoration Day, as it was called in many places, went as far as anything else in shaping southerners' perceptions of their cultural identity.

Decoration Day was quickly adopted around the defeated South. By June 1866, there were graveside commemorations held in at least five Southern states (Virginia, Tennessee, Mississippi, Georgia and South Carolina); by the next year, the custom was regionwide, although the date varied from state to state. In the early years, the event honored those who had given their lives for the Confederacy. As the years passed, it demonstrated love, respect, honor and memory for all those who defended the Confederacy, including the women who remained in their homes and helped produce uniforms, food and other supplies for their soldiers and sustained their families during the hard times of war.

The annual Confederate Memorial Day ritual was one of the key factors that created and perpetuated the Lost Cause. A typical example is the celebration at New Bern, North Carolina, on May 9, 1879. There was a choir, "composed of many of the best voices of the city," and a civic band. Their first number was a "well known requiem" written by a North Carolinian, Mrs. Mary Bayard Clarke. Next was "an appropriate prayer" by Reverend L.C. Vass, and then, another hymn set the stage for Alfred Moore Waddell, a prominent North Carolina political figure, lawyer and journalist, to deliver the oration of the day. Waddell, from Wilmington, North Carolina, had opposed secession but supported his home state and served the Confederacy as a lieutenant colonel. After the war, he was in Congress from 1870 to 1879 and, later, was mayor of Wilmington. Early in his speech, Waddell summed up the Lost Cause and the purpose of Confederate Memorial Day in one paragraph of typically florid and verbose nineteenth-century oratory:

> *Ladies of the Memorial Association: It is customary on these occasions for those who perform the duty assigned to me today, to paint, as best they may, that picture of the past on which Southern eyes will always gaze with admiration, and before which Southern hearts will always throb with mingled pride and sorrow. They try to portray in vivid colors the*

heroism, the splendid courage, the patient toil and suffering, the unselfish patriotism and the sublime devotion of our countrymen who died in an unequal struggle for the preservation of what they believed to be the sacred inheritance of constitutional liberty bequeathed to them by their fathers. The tribute is just, the service is proper, though mortal tongue may vainly strive to form in fitting words the thoughts which such an occasion and such a theme inspire. The season too, is meet, for it is redolent of hope and promise. Not beneath withered branches swaying in the winter wind and amidst dead leaves strewed upon the naked earth shall such services be held; but in the tender spring-time, when to the music of soft winds, odorous with the breath of flowers and gladdened by the songs of birds, transfigured nature makes manifest the miracle of the resurrection. Amidst such surroundings we meet today in this silent city to do honor to the memory of our dead.[7]

The newspaper description of Memorial Day in Norfolk, Virginia, on June 4, 1891, shows the important role the celebration played in the life of this community and across the South: "All day long the streets were thronged with both sexes, while cars to the cemetery were crowded to their utmost capacity, the horses straining with mighty effort to carry the great crowds, which clung to the sides and were packed in the seats, at times staggering and tottering as if they would fall under the great weight."[8]

Another typical Memorial Day commemoration was in Greenville, South Carolina, on May 20, 1890, in which a five o'clock parade of two military units, a cornet band, a "long line of Confederate veterans," a division of students from Furman University, a line of carriages carrying the dignitaries who were to take part in the program, a "brigade of the fair pupils of the Female College and several hundred children from the city graded schools" processed. After placing flowers on the soldiers' graves in the Springwood Cemetery, followed by a salute fired by the military unit, the parade reformed and marched on to the Episcopal Cemetery, where the ceremony was repeated. That night, there was a program at the opera house, in which General Ellison Capers delivered the memorial oration. Capers spoke for "nearly an hour" to a large audience "which crowded the house until there was standing room only."[9]

The women of the South received "a charge" from Jefferson Davis when he wrote the dedication of his two-volume apologia, *The Rise and Fall of the Confederate Government*:

*TO
THE WOMEN OF THE CONFEDERACY,
WHOSE PIOUS MINISTRATIONS TO OUR WOUNDED SOLDIERS
SOOTHED THE LAST HOURS OF THOSE
WHO DIED FAR FROM THE OBJECTS OF THEIR TENDEREST LOVE;
WHOSE DOMESTIC LABORS
CONTRIBUTED MUCH TO SUPPLY THE WANTS OF OUR DEFENDERS IN THE FIELD;
WHOSE ZEALOUS FAITH IN OUR CAUSE SHONE A GUIDING STAR UNDIMMED BY THE
DARKEST CLOUDS OF WAR;
WHOSE FORTITUDE
SUSTAINED THEM UNDER ALL THE PRIVATIONS TO WHICH THEY WERE SUBJECTED;
WHOSE ANNUAL TRIBUTE
EXPRESSES THEIR ENDURING GRIEF, LOVE, AND REVERENCE
FOR OUR SACRED DEAD;
AND WHOSE PATRIOTISM
WILL TEACH THEIR CHILDREN
TO EMULATE THE DEEDS OF OUR REVOLUTIONARY SIRES;
THESE PAGES ARE DEDICATED
BY THEIR COUNTRYMAN,
JEFFERSON DAVIS*

The historian of the Confederated Memorial Associations wrote with some pride about the women of these myriad associations: "Of the early work of the old Memorial Associations too much can not be said. These were the women to whom President Davis referred in his dedication of *The Rise and Fall of the Confederate Government.*"[10] Throughout the South, the women were the leaders in establishing Confederate Memorial Day and promoting the building of Confederate monuments across the region.

The Civil War touched the lives of every American between 1861 and 1965 and for many years afterward. An unprecedented number of citizens fought and died for the reasons they believed to be correct and honorable. In an era before our modern procedures for handling the injured, sick, dying and the dead, thousands of Americans languished in unmarked graves, often far from home and family, never to be found by relatives or friends. In short, the nation, and especially the defeated South, was not prepared to adequately deal with these losses, either of the unknown or all those thousands whose graves could be identified. Memorial Day across the South was a start at dealing with the loss. Arkansas was no different.

CONFEDERATE MONUMENT DEDICATIONS

A second important Lost Cause ritual was the dedication ceremony held at every Confederate monument that was erected in hundreds of communities below Mason's and Dixon's line. By 1912, at least 644 monuments had been erected across the nation, including over 20 in northern states, according to a count by Mrs. B.A.C. Emerson. In an appeal to UDC members to send her photographs and details of the monuments in their areas, Emerson wrote, "These monuments are your heritage. In 1865 you began the work of honoring your fallen heroes by erecting monuments to commemorate their valor and patriotism...how well you have succeeded in this work, a labor of love indeed! At the close of that terrible war on the South our people were impoverished, but not crushed or conquered. They rose in their might and have triumphed."[11] The "triumph" continued; the total number has surpassed 1,000 across our land as we observe the sesquicentennial of the Civil War.

Cheraw, South Carolina, has the honor of having built the first monument to the Confederate soldier. It was placed in the cemetery of St. David Episcopal Church in June 1867. The location was historic, as the church building had been used as a barracks by the British army during the Revolutionary War. The statue is sixteen feet tall, made of Italian marble and cost $1,000—a large sum in the devastated South. Sixty-two Confederate soldiers are buried near the monument.[12]

Each dedication ceremony involved the same essential ingredients: a parade, several brief welcoming addresses by local notables, some musical selections, a poem or two by the local town laureate and the ever-present oration of the day. Finally, the cover was lifted from the monument and the memorial stood as a granite or marble symbol of the Lost Cause. A casual drive through any southern state will show these monuments still exhibited in places of honor, often in the center of town or at the local cemetery where Confederate soldiers had been buried. Wherever they are located, they are surrounded by well-kept grounds and are well maintained by local chapters of the United Daughters of the Confederacy, the local camp of the Sons of Confederate Veterans or the city grounds department. The tie to the past may be tenuous as we proceed through the twenty-first century, but for over one hundred years, these monuments have been visible symbols of the past. Southerners spoke eloquently about Confederate monuments and their role in recalling the past and vindicating the cause that was lost.

Raising money for these monuments was a difficult task in the war-ruined southern economy. Women played the major role in fundraising as the historian of the United Daughters of the Confederacy describes:

> *With homes ruined, and poverty-stricken, these women by selling pies, by having bazaars and ice cream suppers, and little home-talent plays, gathered together nickels and dimes for monuments to their heroes. The dimes grew into dollars, and monuments began to appear. The chapters…have built hundreds and hundreds of monuments, until now nearly every county seat in the South has its Confederate monument in its courthouse square, or on a prominent corner, or in a cemetery—a shrine, a great object lesson to our youth, telling the story of a glorious past, of heroic deeds and unfailing loyalty to a beloved cause.*

The "great object lesson to our youth" was a critical goal of the monument committees, as the UDC fought a major battle for years to ensure that books used in southern schools portrayed the southern point of view, not the winner's point of view; if the monument in the town square could help teach the history of the Confederacy, so much the better.[13]

A typical example of a monument campaign is the one in Pensacola, Florida, for which the women of the community took over a failed attempt by the men to raise money for a monument to be erected in Tallahassee, the state capital. In August 1890, the women organized a ladies' monument association and, three months later, awarded a contract to J.F. Manning of Washington to construct and erect a stone monument for $5,000. It was to honor Edward L. Perry, a Confederate general, and Stephen R. Mallory, secretary of the Confederate navy, both from Pensacola; Jefferson Davis; and "the heroes of the Confederacy." There is an eight-foot figure on top of the column modeled after a painting entitled *Appomattox*, which hung in the old Confederate capitol building in Richmond.

Three thousand visitors came to the Gulf Coast city for the dedication on June 17, 1891. The monument was placed on the hill near the site of Fort George overlooking Pensacola Bay and the downtown area. The park was called Robert E. Lee Square and was decorated with eight hundred thirty-two-pound cannon balls and two old cannons purchased by the women. Off and on since the dedication, debates have flared over the size and location of the park. Over time, it has been reduced in size to accommodate Palafox Street traffic. Today, it is still the scene of an annual observance of Confederate Memorial Day on April 26.[14]

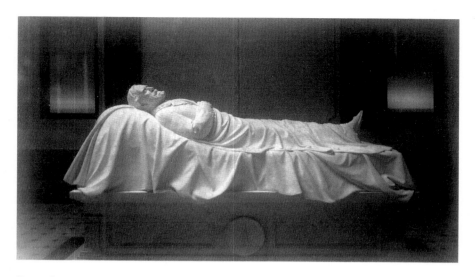

Recumbent statue of Robert E. Lee in Lee Chapel at Washington and Lee University, Lexington, Virginia. *Courtesy of Washington and Lee University Leyburn Library.*

The great folk hero of the Confederacy was Robert E. Lee. Although his armies were eventually crushed by the might of Yankee forces, the gray-clad veterans revered Lee. Many monuments in the defeated region were dedicated to him, and the name of the university where he served as president was changed to honor him. Washington and Lee University also furnished a mausoleum for his body. The "Recumbent Figure" at Lee's Tomb in Lexington "is regarded by authority and held by general acclaim to be one of the grandest works of art in this country," according to a writer in the *Southern Historical Society Papers.*[15]

At the unveiling of Lee's tomb in June 1883, John Warwick Daniel delivered the oration of the day. For three hours, Daniel praised Lee and the Confederacy and held the eight to ten thousand persons in the audience "by the spell of his eloquence, moving it now to applause, and now to tears." Daniel summed up much of the Lost Cause in two sentences: "Robert Edward Lee made fiercer and bloodier fight against greater odds, and at greater sacrifice, and lost—against the greatest nation of modern history, armed with steam and electricity, and all the appliances of modern science; a nation which mustered its hosts at the very threshold of his door. But his life teaches the grandest lesson how manhood can rise transcendent over adversity." Daniel went on to praise Lee's forgiving spirit and called for his audience to do the same: "Lee had nothing in common with the little minds that know not how to forgive. His was the land that had been invaded; his the people who were cut down…his was the cause that perished. He was the General discrowned of his mighty place, and he the citizen disfranchised. Yet Lee forgave, and counseled all to forgive and forget."[16]

The South may have forgiven, but it has not forgotten much about the Civil War.

The most notable concentration of Confederate monuments is Monument Avenue in Richmond, Virginia, the capital of the Confederacy; there are other monuments throughout the city, which has more statues honoring the Confederacy than any other location. A few days after Robert E. Lee's death, a Ladies' Lee Monument

John Warwick Daniel. *Courtesy of the Washington and Lee University Leyburn Library, Lexington, Virginia.*

Association formed with the purpose of raising money for a monument to the beloved Lee. Mrs. William McFarland was elected president, and in spite of the poverty of the South and the continuing devastation of the region as Reconstruction continued, the ladies were highly successful in raising the $15,000 needed for the monument, "a tribute of devotion met by personal sacrifice."[17]

Evidence of the important role of monuments across the South, the 1907 dedication of the Jefferson Davis Monument in Richmond drew 200,000 spectators, "the largest crowd that had ever assembled to honor any aspect of the Confederate cause."[18] In Mississippi, the dedication of the Confederate monument in that state's capital attracted 15,000 to 20,000 southerners and featured a two-mile-long procession through town and an oration by U.S. senator Major General E.C. Walthall.[19]

Historian David W. Blight points out that "monument unveiling days took on a significance equal [to], if not greater than, Memorial Day." It is not difficult to see why that was true, as is indicated in a letter to the editor of the *Confederate Veteran* magazine, the official media of the United Confederate Veterans. In the March 1893 issue, the letter was published in reference to the organization's regionwide appeal for monuments to be built across the South to honor the Confederate soldier, women and the cause. Mrs. Fanny D. Nelson of Aiken, South Carolina, wrote to the editor: "May your success be commensurate with the holy cause you represent." How could a cause considered by Mrs. Nelson, and many other southerners, to be holy, possibly fail?[20]

CONFEDERATE VETERANS' REUNIONS AND ORGANIZATIONS

A third focal point for Lost Cause memory was veterans' organizations and their annual reunions. At first, these meetings were informal, but as the years passed, most of the Confederate military units began to organize, elect officers and hold regularly scheduled annual reunions. At each event, oratory, parades and ceremony were the order of the day. The veterans would gather from where they had limped home after the surrender, and there would be business meetings, election of officers, campfires, barbecues, reminiscences and the usual oratory by southern military leaders—often the wartime commander of the unit.

Most of the reunions across the South were for units that were locally raised by a community or area. By 1889, there was enough regional interest that the United Confederate Veterans was established in New Orleans. Its goals were to help provide for veterans, widows and children of veterans; collect and publish historical materials on the Civil War; educate younger generations about the southern perspective on the war; and create a social force for the friendships established by veterans during the war and after the conclusion of hostilities.

At an early reunion of the UCV, General John B. Gordon, UCV commander, urged the continued growth of the organization:

> *I rejoice that a general organization, too long neglected, has at last been perfected. It is an organization which all honorable men must approve and which heaven itself will bless. I call upon you, therefore, to organize in every State and community where ex-Confederates may reside, and rally to the support of the high and peaceful objects of the United Confederate Veterans, and move forward until by the power of organization and persistent effort your beneficent and Christian purposes are fully accomplished.*[21]

Growth was rapid; in 1898, there were 1,555 local units, called camps, which attended the annual reunion. The membership peaked in 1903 or 1904, after which death began to claim members in rapidly increasing numbers.[22] The last reunion was in 1951 in Norfolk, Virginia.

The United Sons of Confederate Veterans organized at the Richmond UCV reunion in 1896 and, by the turn of the century, could claim over one hundred camps. Its growth continued, and the SCV is still active across the region.[23]

These reunions gained national attention by the last decade of the nineteenth century, and their rhetoric became a major source for the creation and maintenance of the public memory of the war. At the July 1875 reunion of Orr's Rifles in Walhalla, South Carolina, General Samuel McGowan described what he believed was the function of the typical reunion:

> *Let us in peace and in quiet, without malice or hatred to any, hold sweet converse one with another, talk over the past with all its hopes and fears, joys and sorrows, recount the stories of the bivouac and the camp-fire and as we pass, drop a silent tear over the sweet memory of some comrade whom we buried on the battlefield, and recall the long marches and bloody battles in which we suffered and struggled, hungered and toiled, and fought and bled together.[24]*

The reunion was a success, as the local newspaper remarked, "The reunion of the Survivors of Orr's Rifles was everything that the most ardent Confederate and patriotic citizen could wish—no bitterness, no discontent, only a loving pride in the soldiers who fell, a fond recollection of the days that are past, and a fixed determination to be as true to their new allegiance as these brave riflemen were to the cause of the South."[25] The cause may have been lost, but the veterans would do their share in sustaining the memory.

General John B. Gordon delivered a typical reunion oration to the Confederate Survivors' Association in Augusta, Georgia. Gordon was a genuine Confederate hero, possibly second only to Robert E. Lee or Stonewall Jackson in the minds and hearts of many southerners. He attended the University of Georgia, where he was the top orator in his class and had one of the best academic records of his peers. Joining the Confederate forces shortly after the war began, Gordon entered as a captain in the Sixth Alabama and rose to the rank of major general. He was wounded five times at Antietam but returned to action seven months later. When Lee realized further opposition was futile, he selected Gordon to be one of three Confederate generals to negotiate with the Union at Appomattox. In this 1887 speech in Augusta, Gordon developed one of the major themes of the Lost Cause, a picture of the Old South that could have served as the model for Margaret Mitchell as she wrote *Gone with the Wind*, the prewar white South: "It was a civilization where personal courage, personal independence, personal dignity, personal honor, and the manliest virtues were nurtured; where feminine refinement, feminine purity, feminine culture, delicacy, and gentleness express themselves in models of rarest loveliness and perfection; and where, in the language of a great Georgian, 'hospitality was as free and boundless as the vitalizing air around us.'"[26]

These images of the Old South, repeated over and over at these ceremonial events, shaped many white southerners' perceptions and attitudes over what they felt had been lost since the Civil War. The rituals and rhetoric were heard and observed by thousands of southerners and were significant foundation stones in the building of the continuing southern heritage of the Civil War.

2

"IN THE TENDER
SPRING-TIME"

CONFEDERATE MEMORIAL DAY IN ARKANSAS

Citizens of Arkansas were no different from those in other southern states in their desire to select a day to remember their Civil War dead. It is impossible to determine the first Memorial Day event in Arkansas that commemorated the war dead, but because there were so many casualties across the state, we can be sure that this reflective and solemn ceremony was held in many cemeteries in Arkansas. Ladies' Memorial Associations were formed in the larger cities and towns and carried out the same heartfelt tasks as their peers around the region. They sponsored annual events in which many citizens would parade to the local cemetery where Confederates were buried; ceremonies would be held featuring sacred music, prayers, essays and poems written by local women and students; and an oration would be delivered honoring the lives and service of the dead warriors. Then, the community's women and children would place their homemade wreaths and bouquets of flowers at every Confederate gravesite. Often, baskets of food would be brought to the cemetery, and the participants would enjoy a "dinner on the grounds" for which many would stay to eat and visit with one another before beginning the walk back into town.

The most influential Arkansas memorial association was formed in Fayetteville on June 10, 1872, the Southern Memorial Association (SMA) of Washington County, Arkansas. The SMA's "38 earnest workers" planned from the beginning to purchase land for a cemetery in which to reinter hundreds of Confederate soldiers who had been killed at the battles of Pea Ridge, Prairie Grove, Fayetteville and Cane Hill or who had died in the area from illness. As was the case throughout the South, many Confederates had been buried in quickly dug graves and many in mass graves with few identifying markers; the SMA was determined to provide proper burials in the area. Auxiliary groups were formed at Prairie Grove, Cane Hill and Springdale, and they provided assistance to the Fayetteville organization. The SMA president, Lizzie Pollard, summed up the role of the association: "We have our dead here from the battle-fields of Pea Ridge, Prairie Grove, from Hospitals, from skirmish-ground, from road-side and fence-corner—just where they laid their burdens down."[27]

The organization's declared purpose was to obtain an appropriate site for the burial of Confederate dead, properly maintain the cemetery, build a wall around it and improve the setting with shrubbery and trees.

About three acres in an octagonal shape were acquired and enclosed with a fence on the side of East Mountain in Fayetteville. The grounds were divided into eight triangular sections with their apex at the center of the cemetery. Four of the triangles were each assigned for the graves of soldiers from Texas, Arkansas, Missouri and Louisiana and four for ornamental shrubbery. At the head of the Missouri section is the grave of General W.Y. Slade, who was killed at Pea Ridge. His reburial occurred on Decoration Day in 1880. Again, it was a "drizzly day," but thousands attended the ceremony. From the beginning, plans were developed to mount a statue at the center of the grounds, and although it took twenty-five years, that mission was accomplished, as we will see in chapter three.

The members were expected to attend all meetings of the SMA. A motion in 1872 called for "all who fail to attend a regular meeting except in case of sickness be fined 10 cents"; it passed unanimously and was later incorporated into the bylaws of the group's constitution. These women were serious about their business as well. Another bylaw stated, "There be no sewing or side conversations during business" and that no one speak "except to the president." The members were also warned that anyone "indulging in loud talking or laughter during business hours shall be fined the sum of five cents."

When the cemetery was dedicated one year after the founding of the Southern Memorial Association, the ceremony drew an estimated audience of three thousand persons. An observer called it the "largest crowd ever assembled in the county since the burial of Col. Archibald Yell," a former Arkansas governor. In that first year, several hundred Confederates, most of whom had been killed at Pea Ridge and Prairie Grove, had been reinterred. Local businesses closed from 10:00 a.m. to 3:00 p.m., and there was a mile-long parade on a rainy day to the cemetery. A Mr. Henry had been contracted to bring reburials to the cemetery at $1.40 for each body brought from Pea Ridge and $2.50 for each reburial from other places around northwest Arkansas. This fee included the casket and the burial. Three hundred bodies had been reinterred, and a pine-plank fence erected around the 3.48 acres.

In his dedication address, Reverend (Major) Fontaine R. Earle defined the purpose of the ceremony: "The men whose remains are gathered here were Southern soldiers. As such, they went to war, as such they endured the heat and cold, as such they fought and fell in many a battlefield, and as such we honor them." Part of that honor was the laying of flowers on the graves by children as the commemoration drew to a close. In the early years, the ceremony filled the biggest part of the day, and families would bring a meal and spread it out for the family and their friends. The events were similar to family reunions in many ways but were always held in a solemn and reverent, church-like mood, as can be expected, due to the setting and the memories of the dead.

In the years of economic struggles across the South, the SMA labored to raise the necessary money to carry out its vision. During the first year, it hosted a supper at a local hotel, and the banquet and concert by the Fayetteville band netted $174.55 for its coffers. A "Tableaux and Charades" at McIlroy's Hall; a "Fair," at which they auctioned a "fine piano," sofa cushions, a quilt, a "handsome" oil pointing by local art teacher Sally Bryant and a lock of General Lee's hair; a concert at "Botefuhr and Springer's Hall"; and a "Fair" during the Christmas season brought in more money. The auxiliary groups around the area made donations, and the SMA solicited funds from residents in Texas, Louisiana, Missouri and around Arkansas, as those were the home states of the soldiers to be buried in the cemetery. This appeal brought in an $86.80 donation from the "ladies of Gainesville, Texas," as well as other contributions.

The expenses of the SMA continued, of course, as a few examples of fundraising efforts will demonstrate. On the Fourth of July in 1873, a "Moonlight Festival" was held in Mr. White Walker's grove of trees decorated with paper lanterns. In 1877, a New Year's reception was held where homemade prizes were fished from an indoor "well." In 1879, a concert, tableaux and a drama called "The Forest Rose" was held at Reed and Ferguson's Hall. Fayetteville was not the only location to enjoy these fundraising events. In 1896, the newspaper reported, "A program of exercises will be given at the public school building in Prairie Grove on Friday, Feb. 26, in the interest of the Confederate Dead." The agenda included music by the

Prairie Grove band, a recitation by Miss MayBelle Adams, a lecture by Major F.R. Earle, "The Confederate Soldier" and several other presentations.

Twenty-six years after the founding of the SMA, Lizzie Pollard wrote in the United Confederate Veterans' magazine, *Confederate Veteran*, about the fundraising efforts and the purpose to which the funds were put:

> *All this has cost us many thousand dollars. Much of this money, most of it, is the fruit of actual labor; all of it the offspring of steady and fixed purpose of faithful and unwavering energy, of true and unfaltering love for the memory of the heroes of the "Lost Cause." We have annually called together friends and comrades and paid fitting tribute to our dead. This custom we will endeavor to leave as a sacred heritage to our children to teach them that these were men who, "true to the instincts of their birth, faithful to the teachings of their fathers, died in the performance of their duty." We make this tribute in loving reverence to true courage and heroism—a tribute to the valor of men who knew how to fight, who knew how to die for principle.*[28]

There were continual improvements to the property. In 1885, a stone wall replaced the plank fence. Trees were planted in memory of Confederate soldiers. An iron gate with stone posts was built in 1926, and a gazebo was built in 1980. In 2001, storms damaged the monument, but it was quickly repaired and rededicated in 2002. In 2004, the rock wall was repaired. The Fayetteville Confederate Cemetery is "among the few in the South dedicated solely to the Confederate dead," and the SMA remains active in 2013 by maintaining the cemetery and hosting Confederate Memorial Day ceremonies on the second Saturday in June each year. The cemetery is on the National Register of Historic Places; therefore, the SMA has a reason to maintain and preserve the site in all appropriate ways in order to ensure that the cemetery will remain on this prestigious listing. The SMA also owns the nearby Walker Cemetery, and the organization has pledged to maintain its historic legacy as well (it was placed on the National Register in 2012). The SMA is a nonprofit, tax-exempt organization, and all donations for the care of the Confederate Cemetery and the Walker Cemetery are tax deductible.

By 1903, there were marble markers placed at each grave. At the memorial services on June 3, 1903, with the new markers upgrading the appearance of the cemetery, veterans marched to the monument, and each was handed a green wreath to place on a grave of a fallen Confederate. Colonel Charles

Above: Confederate Cemetery Memorial: Annual Memorial Ceremony, Fayetteville, circa 1900s. *Courtesy Shiloh Museum of Ozark History/Washington County Historical Society Collection (P-189).*

Opposite, bottom: Confederate Memorial Day Parade, Fayetteville. *Courtesy Shiloh Museum of Ozark History/Bob Besom Collection (S-82-78-28).*

Coffin of Walnut Ridge was the main orator of the day and was well into his speech when rain began to fall. He wanted to stop and let his audience seek shelter, but he was compelled to continue as his listeners shouted, "Go on, we want to hear you." As the reporter wrote, it was a "tribute to the speaker and his subject."

The Southern Memorial Association of Washington County became the core organization for a regionwide association of similar groups when, in 1900, Miss Sue Walker, the SMA's corresponding secretary, sent out an appeal for memorial organizations to meet in Louisville, Kentucky, with the United Confederate Veterans on May 30. The group presented a memorial regarding its founding and asking for the support of the UCV and permission to meet concurrently with the UCV annual reunion. Colonel Charles Coffin of Arkansas read the memorial, which read in part: "Many of us are veterans—veterans as much as the gray, battle-scarred old soldiers, tho' we bided at home. While they stood amid the smoke of battle, we stood amid the smoke of burning homes; when they fought, we wept and prayed; when they were hungry, we had only a crust at home; when their clothes were wearing thru [*sic*] on the long and weary march, we were busy with wheel and loom and needles; when they were in peril on picket, we held tearful, prayerful vigils. Are we not veterans as well as they?" How could the soldiers have turned away that petition? It was accepted unanimously.

That meeting of thirteen associations from around the South at the Galt House Hotel marked the creation of the Confederated Southern Memorial Associations. Those thirteen groups had expanded to twenty-three by that fall, when the organization was chartered in Fayetteville on October 30. The idea caught on quickly, and in four years, there were sixty-two memorial associations with an average membership of seventy-five ladies. The organizations were described as "very active and zealous…engaging in various types of memorial work." In the 1940s, there were between eighty and ninety active chapters around the South, some meeting with local United Daughters of the Confederacy chapters.

The work of these memorial associations created a heritage that is strong today. Donna Schwieder, Fayetteville's SMA president in 2012, wrote that she cared about the Confederate Cemetery for the same reasons as those who founded the organization over a century before: "I wish to continue the goal of the founding ladies, to preserve a beautiful resting place for the men in gray who defended hearth and home from an invading army." In the twenty-first century, around eighty members agree with her sentiments as they continue the heritage of the Confederate Cemetery in Fayetteville.

OTHER MEMORIAL ORGANIZATIONS AND CEMETERIES IN ARKANSAS

There were other memorial organizations that established and maintained cemeteries and promoted Confederate Memorial Day across the state. In some cases, the memorial work was carried out by the local chapters of the United Daughters of the Confederacy. Whatever the vehicle, the Confederate soldier was carefully commemorated throughout Arkansas.

The Van Buren organization took the name of the Ladies' Southern Memorial Association when it formed on June 2, 1875. Soon after its creation, the city gave a plot in the city cemetery to the organization for 460 Confederate soldiers who died in the area or who were brought to Van Buren from Texas, Louisiana, Missouri, the Indian Territory or elsewhere in Arkansas.[29]

In Little Rock, Oakland Cemetery was the burial ground of many Confederates. Around nine hundred, many of whom died in hospitals in Little Rock, are buried in graves where two or three are interred together, wrapped in blankets. The Ladies' Memorial Association placed a "stone coping with a tablet stating the estimated number," but it is impossible to locate many of the graves. In another part of Oakland Cemetery, about six hundred Confederates are buried in a section that was neglected and overgrown until 1884, when a memorial association formed "to erect a monument and care for these graves." Mrs. Mary Fields was elected the president of the association, which built a stone wall and erected an iron gate. No names were ever located, and the tombstones are marked only with numbers. Some soldiers originally buried in Mount Holly Cemetery were reinterred in Oakland with a mound over their resting place. In the early years of the twentieth century, bones were found when a new street was being constructed near Oakland, and they were reburied in the Confederate section. This memorial association became the Memorial Chapter of the United Daughters of the Confederacy, and into the early part of the twentieth century, it cared for the cemetery.

In Washington, the wartime capital of the state, an act of the legislature in 1888 created a cemetery where seventy-four Confederate soldiers who died there are buried. Most are thought to have been from Missouri and Texas. A record was kept by a Confederate soldier. But he moved from the area, and the records have not been found. The ruling elders of the Presbyterian Church of Washington are the local trustees of the cemetery.

Clarksville's Oakland Cemetery was the burial ground of about 170 unknown Confederate dead who were interred in the cemetery owned by the Methodist Church. Their bodies were taken up and reinterred in a square plot. The United Daughters of the Confederacy placed a small, unlettered marble headstone at each grave and a curb around the plot. The Methodist Church gave the ladies of Clarksville management of the plot.

The Camden cemetery is near the campgrounds used by troops of Generals Marmaduke and Price, and over 250 of their soldiers were buried there. Only 50 could be identified, and their headstones were marked. "Confederate Soldier" was engraved on those for whom identification could not be certain. A memorial association was formed, and Decoration Day

Speakers' stand at Confederate Section in Little Rock National Cemetery. *Courtesy of W. Stuart Towns.*

was held on November 9, 1866. An account of the cemetery notes that there are other graves of veterans scattered around the cemetery as well as graves of those who lived in the area after the war, who "when death called were buried here beside their comrades."

There are over three hundred unmarked Confederate graves in a military cemetery contiguous to the Fort Smith military post. Most of these soldiers died at Fort Smith, Oak Hill, Prairie Grove and Pea Ridge. Some time before 1908, the United Daughters of the Confederacy bought a plot in the city cemetery that was used for the burial of soldiers as they died in the early twentieth century.

A major Confederate burial ground is at Camp Nelson in Lonoke County, near Cabot. After the James Adams Camp of the United Confederate Veterans was formed in 1897, the commander, T.J. Young, learned of a large burial of four to five hundred Confederate soldiers near a large spring where General Nelson's Texas Cavalry and other units camped for a period of time. The troops were hit by a measles epidemic, and the victims were buried near the spring. The UCV members tried to raise money but were not successful, so they went to the Arkansas legislature and received a $1,000 appropriation in 1905 for the purpose of establishing a Confederate Cemetery at Camp

Nelson. The cemetery "was dedicated with appropriate ceremonies" on October 9, 1906.

After that auspicious start, the cemetery was badly neglected until the 1980s, when local students and their teachers restored the cemetery and rededicated it in April 1982. The Arkansas Department of Parks and Tourism provided a $23,000 grant for the restoration and upkeep of the cemetery and monument. The Veteran's Administration replaced the original stones marking the reinterred bodies with white granite markers. These markers are not at the precise locations of the burials, as the original interments were in several mass graves.[30]

One of the most important Arkansas battles of the Civil War occurred in Helena on July 4, 1863. The city of Helena has commemorated its connection to the war in many ways, one of which is the Confederate Cemetery. The burial ground is at the top of Crowley's Ridge, overlooking the Mississippi River in the southeast corner of the Maple Hill Cemetery. In May 1869, the Phillips County Memorial Association was formed at Phillips Academy, fourteen miles west of Helena, and a branch was organized in Helena. The purpose of the organization was to "care for the Confederate dead and decorate their graves." Mrs. John T. Jones of Lexa was elected president, and Miss Mary Moore Lambert was the vice-president. The memorial association collected the remains of "hundreds of dead soldiers who were buried in haste after the battle of Helena" and reinterred them in the burial grounds on a "beautiful plateau, upon a wooded hillside." The plateau is still beautiful and heavily wooded around the Confederate plot. There are also historical markers and two monuments, one to General Patrick Cleburne of Helena and the other to Confederate soldiers. There is also a monument at the burial site of General Thomas Hindman, but it is not in the Confederate section of the cemetery.[31]

Another cemetery bearing eighty-five unknown Confederate soldiers' graves, buried five to a tomb, is located near Rondo, just east of Texarkana, Arkansas. The soldiers were thought to have died from an epidemic that swept through their nearby camp.[32]

In Hot Springs, there is a Confederate lot in Hollywood Cemetery that was purchased by North Carolina Confederate soldier David Stone Ryan, who had moved to the city in 1900. Before he died in 1907, Ryan deeded the plot to the local United Daughters of the Confederacy chapter, and it holds a memorial ceremony at this location. The lot is sixty feet by fifty-four feet and is surrounded by a low concrete wall. It has been on the National Register of Historic Places since 1996.[33]

Unknown Confederate burials in Rondo Cemetery. *Courtesy of W. Stuart Towns.*

Reverend James B. Evans of Hot Springs gave the following classic Memorial Day oration at the Confederate lot on May 9, 1954, to the assembled UDC:

> *This sacred Sabbath, the early spring, we come to this hallowed spot where rest the remains of the South's heroes who are dear to us. The memory of their struggle is daguerreotyped upon our hearts. Their battle of carnage, their deeds of valor are sacred.*
>
> *Their years of struggle were not alone a war to retain slavery, but a justice and principle in a forced edict.*
>
> *It was a sad hour when Gen. Lee faced Gen. Grant upon the fields of Appomattox while soldiers stood with bowed heads and the Stars and Bars bowed to the Stars and Stripes. The war was ended. We were again one nation and one people.*
>
> *Returning to their homes they began anew the labors of reconstruction. Homes wrecked by the plowshare of war, yet around each sacred hearth gathered courageous souls to rebuild upon the asked crust of desolation a new South.*
>
> *Today we honor their valor and upon their tombs place these tokens of our adoration and love—to their ideals of justice.*

*God give us the spirit to consecrate our lives to our nation, as a whole, as
they did their lives to the South in their hour of conflict.*

*It may be now a new South with ringing wheels of commerce, moving
traffic, and commercial transactions. It may be a beehive of industry
with skyscrapers, railroads, and concrete highways—yet with all this
advancement the scar of the spear is still in her side and the prints of the
nails in the hands.*

May God bless the South and may God bless the Nation.[34]

Yet another Confederate cemetery in the state is in the small community
of Sulphur Springs in Jefferson County, near Pine Bluff. Camp White
Sulphur Springs was a staging area for volunteers who came from the area to
join the Confederate forces. When troops from Texas and Indian Territory
(Oklahoma) came into the area, they created an epidemic of measles and
smallpox, and somewhere between 150 and 175 died. They were buried
in the camp area or near the hotel, which was turned into a hospital. The
Pine Bluff camp of the Sons of Confederate Veterans began a campaign
in the 1980s with the David O. Dodd chapter of the United Daughters of
the Confederacy to restore the cemetery and identify the graves. In 1994,
they began to place headstones, and in 1996, the SCV and UDC made an
agreement to build fencing, flagpoles and historical markers in the cemetery.
It was listed on the National Register of Historic Places on January 19, 2005.
Since 1997, the UDC and SCV have sponsored a memorial service for the
soldiers interred in the cemetery on the second weekend in October.[35]

A typical memorial Decoration Day was similar to the one held in
Lonoke and conducted by the United Daughters of the Confederacy on
May 26, 1912. The newspaper notice pointed out that veterans, sons of
veterans and friends were all welcome to the ceremony, which was to be held
at the Methodist Church at 2:30 p.m. Mrs. W.Y. Bransford was collecting
all the flowers that would be taken to the cemetery to decorate the graves
after the program at the church. The program included an invocation, the
song "Sewanee River," a Confederate soldier's letter being read, a solo by
Miss Elle Mae Fletcher, a reading about General Robert E. Lee by Pattie
Griffin, a male quartette rendering of "Sleep Kentucky Babe," an oration
by Reverend Boles and a closing song, "Old Black Joe." The march to the
cemetery was led by Dixie Beard and David P. Dodd, followed by veterans,
daughters, sons of Confederates and friends.[36]

As we can see from this survey of Confederate Memorial Day
commemorations and the creation and maintaining of Confederate

Confederate Cemetery at Sulphur Springs. *Courtesy of W. Stuart Towns.*

Lest We Forget. *Courtesy of W. Stuart Towns.*

cemeteries across Arkansas, those families whose heritages include Confederate soldiers who died in the Civil War can rest assured that their kinfolk's last resting place is being protected and maintained by other southerners who care about that heritage and tradition. Although the South did not have nationally sponsored cemeteries, the Confederate soldiers had the women of the Confederated Southern Memorial Association and the United Daughters of the Confederacy, as well as the United Confederate Veterans and the Sons of Confederate Veterans, who expended much time, money and effort to ensure the protection of Confederate dead. As many a southern monument, marker or tombstone reads in memory of the Confederate soldier: "Lest We Forget." Those who survived the war, those who followed them and many today whose family's heritage was touched by the war did not forget and, as we can suspect, will not forget the heroism and courage of those who died.

3

ON THE MONUMENT TRAIL

BUILDING THE HERITAGE IN STONE

Why have monuments been an integral part of human culture since history has been recorded? They have recorded in stone part of the story of our history, and for many generations, they help tell us, at least partly, how we see ourselves as a people. They bring back memories of how we recall who we are and the heritage and traditions of our cultures, our landscapes, our communities, our families and ourselves. A study of ancient Egypt, Greece, the Roman world and just about any other known national entity would not be complete without a focus on their memorial statuary and art.

A brief personal story will illustrate the important role of war memorials and monuments. On a recent trip to Washington, D.C., I walked to the World War II Memorial on the National Mall between the Capitol and the Lincoln Memorial. While strolling around the monument reading the various inscriptions regarding the theaters of the war, three large tour buses pulled up and unloaded their passengers: dozens of World War II veterans and their escorts. Many were in wheelchairs; others walked with canes. All had a somber and reverent air about them as they moved into the memorial. I watched carefully as they became involved with what they were reading, talking softly about it and remembering—perhaps for the first time in many years. Without exception, they were immersed in the memorial. Before I left, about the time some were beginning to board the buses for their next tour stop, I saw many of the veterans wiping tears from their eyes as they read and thought and talked about what the memorial was telling them.

Although no one is left who fought in the Civil War, memorials to the fallen and the battles of the defeated Confederate States of America can tell part of the story of the South and southerners—both white and black. The Civil War helped to shape America and the South in so many ways, and visiting these monuments and memorials, studying and understanding that defining four years of our history, will help us understand better what that most terrible war meant to our nation. We cannot escape that history or change or ignore it. Stone and bronze monuments are an aid to our remembering—and we cannot, must not, forget our history.

Arkansas is no different in this regard. We have honored and memorialized our soldiers of all our wars from the Revolution through our current conflicts in Iraq and Afghanistan with monuments, markers, roadside displays and battlefield site preservations all across the state. Many of the most noticeable are the memorials to the Confederate soldiers and the women of the Confederacy. A 1911 compilation of Confederate monuments around the nation showed 644, with 24 in Arkansas.[37] There are over 50 in 2013.

My count indicates Arkansas is home to at least fifty-three Confederate memorials of one kind or another: boulders with brass plaques identifying or discussing some element of the conflict; classical obelisks and statues of Confederate soldiers or women of the Confederacy; and memorials to specific heroes, such as General Patrick Cleburne or David O. Dodd, or simply, "To Our Confederate Dead." This list does not include the roadside markers being erected by the Arkansas Civil War Sesquicentennial Commission's program to place at least one marker in each of Arkansas's seventy-five counties by the end of the sesquicentennial in 2015. It also does not include markers or interpretive signs placed on battlefields or other locations explaining what happened at that spot during or after the war or any of the roadside markers placed during the centennial observance of the Civil War in 1961–65.

I am organizing this statewide discussion of Confederate monuments into five geographical sections of the state: northeast, southeast, southwest, northwest and central Arkansas. This organization will be helpful for those readers who may want to take a day trip or make a weekend visit to some of these sites, as it conforms to the way the state is divided on the Department of Parks and Tourism's Civil War Trails map, which I discuss in chapter five. It is my hope that this discussion of these memorials will encourage you to visit, ponder and reflect on our history as Arkansans, southerners and Americans.

MONUMENTS IN ARKANSAS'S NORTHEAST

Batesville was the first city in northeast Arkansas to erect a monument to the soldiers of the Confederacy. The planning began in the summer of 1906, when the Sidney Johnston Chapter 135 of the United Daughters of the Confederacy and the Sidney Johnston Camp 863 of the United Confederate Veterans established a joint committee to develop the plans for the monument. The committee was composed of Mr. Robert Neill, Mrs. Lara C. Ewing, Stevadson A. Hail, Mrs. Kate Hooper, James P. Coffin and Mrs. Emily Reed. Within two months, they had agreed on a design by Leo Pfeiffer and had awarded the contract to Mr. Otto Pfeiffer, who owned a marble quarry about six miles from Batesville. The committee selected the location at the corner of Broad and Main Streets, on the northwest corner of the Independence County courthouse lawn. Pfeiffer completed the monument in January 1907. It was accepted, and the committee paid $831.40 to the Pfeiffers, which included preparing the ground and installing the monument.

The monument has engravings on all four sides. On the front is recorded:

In Memory of
The Sons of Independence County
Who served in the
Confederate Army,
Their Mothers, Wives, Sisters, and Daughters,
Who, with patriotic devotion,
Remained steadfast to their cause
During the
War Period
1861–1865

On the Broad Street side are the names of the ten companies of cavalry, and on the opposite side are the names of the thirteen companies of infantry that enlisted from Independence County. The various officers who commanded these twenty-three companies are also listed. On the back face are the names of the veterans' camp and the descendants' organization and their "many friends" who directed and sponsored the creation of the monument.

May 1, 1907, was the day appointed for the dedication; the night before, the honored guest, U.S. senator James H. Berry, was treated to a reception,

Dedication of Confederate monument on the Batesville Courthouse lawn. *Courtesy of Old Independence Regional Museum, Batesville, Powell-Guard Collection.*

which, according to one report, was decorated with "Confederate flags… in profusion."

On May Day, Senator Berry, who was commander of the Arkansas Division of the United Confederate Veterans, and Robert G. Shaver, who had commanded two Arkansas regiments in the war, were the featured speakers at the "impressive ceremony." Independence County soldiers had served in both of Shaver's regiments.

The Albert Sidney Johnston Chapter 135 of the UDC and the Job S. Neill Camp 286, Sons of Confederate Veterans, celebrated its one-hundred-year anniversary and rededicated it on November 3, 2007.[38]

About twenty-four miles southeast from Batesville on AR 14 is the former county seat of Jackson County, Jacksonport. The site is an Arkansas State Park, and along with the well-restored county courthouse, now a museum, is the Confederate monument, originally placed in 1914 at Newport, just across the river. After being moved several times, the county seat was placed in Jacksonport. It was located at the confluence of the White and Black Rivers, so it became a major trade center from the 1850s through the 1880s. The courthouse was completed in 1872.

Unfortunately for Jacksonport, the Cairo and Fulton Railroad went through Newport, and the county seat refused to build a $25,000 spur from the main line across the river. The decline of the town began soon thereafter, and Newport became the leading community in Jackson County. After two elections failed to move the county seat across the river, the third time was the charm, and an election in 1892 moved the courthouse to Newport.

The monument campaign was spearheaded by William Edwin Bevens of Newport, whose "untiring efforts" led to the funding from private donations. He wrote a book, *Reminiscences of a Private*, which he sold for $1.00 a copy, primarily to help fund the monument. Bevens wrote to the *Confederate Veteran* in 1922: "We have a fine monument in our courthouse yard to the memory of the Confederate dead of Jackson County…We are very proud of our monument." After he became the last surviving member of the Jackson Guards, Bevens continued to visit the memorial every year and place a wreath on the monument.

The Jackson Guards Memorial was dedicated on November 25, 1914, at the courthouse in Newport. The unveiling was attended by an "immense audience," according to the *Newport Daily Independent*. The monument is about twenty-five feet tall, and a Confederate soldier statue stands at ease at the top. The engravings on the memorial tell much of the story of the Jackson Guards, including a list of its commissioned and noncommissioned officers and a full list of its enlisted members. Each name has a symbol that indicates if that soldier was wounded, discharged, killed, transferred, died, furnished substitute or was detailed to another unit. The monument also has an engraved list of the battles in which the Jackson Guards fought, which includes First Manassas, Shiloh, Chickamauga, Missionary Ridge, Franklin and Nashville, among others.

The program at the unveiling included a chorus by public school children, signing the "Bonnie Blue Flag," some introductory remarks by Bevens and the oration of the day by Junius Jordan of Pine Bluff. The unveiling was done by Lady Elizabeth Watson—granddaughter of Major General James Fagan, a Confederate division commander—and Clare Phillips, granddaughter of Robert Neill, captain in the First Arkansas Mounted Riflemen. The event ended with a school children's chorus of "Dixie."

The statue remained in Newport until the 1960s, when efforts began to save the long-abandoned courthouse building. The Jackson County Historical Society, led by Lady Elizabeth Luker, was formed in 1962, and renovation of the courthouse at Jackson was undertaken. In 1965, the area was designated an Arkansas State Park featuring the restored courthouse and the Confederate monument, which was moved from Newport in 1965. As part of the centennial commemoration of the 1865 surrender of 6,000 Confederate troops at Jacksonport, the monument was moved and

Confederate soldier monument at Jacksonport State Park. *Courtesy of W. Stuart Towns.*

rededicated on June 5, 1965. Governor Orval E. Faubus was the speaker of the day, and the event was attended by an audience estimated at 2,500. A marker describing the surrender and the newly created state park were also dedicated as part of the ceremonies.

A tornado damaged the park on March 1, 1997, and the courthouse and the *Mary Woods No. 2*, a paddleboat built in 1931, were closed until March 2002. The reopening ceremony was held on May 14, 2002, and featured Governor Mike Huckabee.[39]

About forty-five miles southwest of Jacksonport is the city of Searcy, the county seat of White County. A large statue sits on the corner of the courthouse lawn. The efforts of the local United Daughters of the Confederacy chapter, under the leadership of Mrs. Richard B. Willis, were responsible for the creation of the statue of a Confederate soldier. The ladies were proud of the fact that they raised the money through public subscription, as that was noted in the inscription on the monument: "Erected to the Memory of the Confederate Soldiers of White County by Public Subscription 1917."

After a reunion in Searcy's Spring Park, the county's Confederate veterans marched to the courthouse square for the unveiling of the monument. A local band accompanied the marchers to the site. The ceremonies were held in the courtroom on a level with the head of the statue outside. The widow of General Dandridge McRae read the 100th Psalm, and the orator of the day was Stephen Brundidge, who "thrilled the old veterans' hearts with a Southern account of the cause and course of the war with which they were familiar." He went further and praised the former Confederates for their role in rebuilding the devastated region after the war and claimed that the Reconstruction effort was the "marvel of the civilized world." Brundidge, like most of the dedicatory speakers at similar events around the South, affirmed his belief that the South was correct in its stand that led to the war, but he emphasized his love of the Union. The nation had just entered World War I, and calls for national unity and support were sweeping the country. The ranks were thinning rapidly, as fifteen veterans had died in the year since their 1916 reunion. The monument is on the National Register of Historic Places.[40]

The remaining memorials in the northeast section of Arkansas take the form of smaller "boulder" monuments, which honor the Confederacy in a simpler fashion than the large statue or obelisk form. The reason for this difference is impossible to determine, but the postwar economic situation of the region might be to blame; few communities could afford the cost

Confederate monument on the White County Courthouse lawn in Searcy. *Courtesy of the Old Independence Regional Museum.*

of a major monument. Another reason could be that the northeast part of the state was, perhaps, the area with more pro-Union support than any other region of Arkansas. As Nancy Britton of the Independence County Historical Society suggested in an e-mail: "I think it is misleading for serious historians to write and teach in a way that implies that everyone in North Arkansas was (and is) strongly Confederate—pro-slavery and anti-Union." She also points out that Independence County had a "pretty strong undercover Union sentiment before and during the war."

These Union feelings are illustrated by the presence in Judsonia, just north of Searcy, of one of only four monuments in Arkansas honoring Union soldiers. This large memorial was erected in 1894 by the W.T. Sherman Post No. 84 of the Grand Army of the Republic and is located in the Evergreen Cemetery. There are sixteen Union veterans buried close to the monument. It is one of only two in the state erected by the GAR; the other one is in Siloam Springs.[11]

Mississippi County is one of the few counties in the state that has two county seats: Blytheville and Osceola. Both courthouse lawns are graced with Confederate boulder-type monuments. They are very similar in size, shape and inscription on each plaque. According to a 1960 compilation of information and descriptions of Confederate monuments and markers in the state, the Blytheville monument is made from red Missouri granite, and the Osceola monument is from red sandstone. Both are described as being about six feet long and four feet high. They were both dedicated at the time of the 1934 Convention of the Arkansas Division of the United Daughters of the Confederacy that was held in Blytheville. The inscriptions on both read:

> 1861 [*Laurel wreath and flag insignia*] 1865
> In Memory
> Of the
> Confederate Veterans
> Of
> Mississippi County
> Erected A.D. 1934
> United Daughters of the Confederacy
> Elliott Fletcher Chapter
> Blytheville, Arkansas[12]

Crittenden County is just to the south of Mississippi County and has two Confederate memorials of its own. One is a boulder monument in front of the courthouse in Marion, which is just east of I-55, at exit 10. It is a granite marker somewhat smaller than its counterparts to the north, measuring about four feet by four feet in size. The metal tablet reads:

1861   1865
In Memory of
Crittenden County's
Confederate Soldiers
Erected By
Crittenden County Chapter UDC
October 1936[13]

Also at the courthouse in Marion is a unique memorial. A historical marker points out that the magnolia trees on that spot were planted in memory of Confederate soldiers; no date is given, but one can assume that it was on or about the October 4, 1936 dedication of the boulder monument a few feet away. One of the trees has a small plaque on the ground beneath it that points out that tree was planted for "Maj. R.F. Crittenden for his service in Arms, 1846–1899."

Another small memorial is in Crawfordsville, ten miles west of Marion on U.S. 64. This one is a unique iron marker set in concrete and placed by the same Crittenden County Chapter of the UDC. It is located on Old Highway 64, just east of the downtown area in a vacant lot in a residential area. The metal plaque reads:

Crawfordsville
Named for Adolphus Fountain
Crawford
Born Aug. 15, 1848
Died Feb. 21, 1876
Confederate Soldier of Arkansas
He Fought Under Gen. Price
This Marker Was Erected by the
Crittenden County Chapter
of the
United Daughters of the Confederacy
1938[44]

On the left side of Cross County Road 367, southeast of Vanndale in Cross County, there is a boulder monument on Crowley's Ridge near Pineville. This memorial is only two and a half feet high by two and a half feet long and one and a half feet thick. Twelve Confederate veterans were present at the unveiling, as well as the president of the Arkansas Division, United Daughters of the Confederacy, Mrs. Lora Gaines Goolsby. Judge Driver of Osceola and George Moreland of Memphis were the speakers for the dedication event on July 30, 1926. There was a Civil War Centennial commemoration ceremony at the site on June 11, 1961, one hundred years after Company A, Fifth Regiment, Arkansas Volunteers, was mobilized on June 13, 1861.[45]

Another marker in the northeast section of the state was located near Cotton Plant and served to commemorate the Battle of Cotton Plant—or, as it is sometimes called, Cache River. It is a boulder monument about five feet tall. It was originally located on the site of the July 7, 1861 battle, on what is called by the compiler of the records the "old Hill Plantation." It was reduced in size and moved to the front lawn of the Cotton Plant Post Office some time after its original placement. The bronze plaque is inscribed:

July 7, 1862, The 11th Wisconsin
Infantry Of The Federals Commanded By
Colonel Hovey, Met The Confederate Texas
Cavalry Commanded By General Rust At
Hill's Plantation And Engaged In A Bitter
Fight.
The Battle Of Cache River Or
Cotton Plant Is Conceded By The Federals
To Have Been One Of The Most Remarkable
And Hard Fought Battles Of The War Between
The States.
Cotton Plant Chapter
United Daughters Of The Confederacy[46]

Monuments in Arkansas's Southeast

Moving into the southeast section of the state, we find more of the traditional statuesque monuments. Marianna will be our first stop at the City Square, where General Robert E. Lee, the namesake of Lee County, is memorialized. The park, a two-acre plot, was the creation of a ladies' Civic Improvement League that planned and landscaped the area, built a $300 bandstand and erected the Lee Monument in its center. A marble shaft is topped with a life-size statue of Lee carved from Italian marble. The inscription on the front of the monument reads:

> Erected by
> D.C. Govan Chapter
> UDC
> In Loving Memory of
> Lee County's
> Confederate
> Soldiers
> No Braver Bled For a
> Brighter Land
> No Brighter Land Had
> Cause So Grand

Other inscriptions on each of the other three sides praise the Southern soldier's bravery and fortitude and conclude with, "Their memories e'er shall remain for us and their names, bright names, without stain for us. Our Heroes in Gray."

The Lee Monument was dedicated on December 8, 1910, on an "unpleasantly cold" day, but the "biting climatic conditions existing Thursday morning did in nowise dampen the ardor and loyalty of the old veterans or the sons and daughters of the Old South, or did it prevent them from turning out in large numbers to witness the unveiling of the Lee statue." The large audience observed a ceremony that was "impressive in its simplicity and expressive in its solemnity," according to the local newspaper. When the statue was unveiled, the local band played "Dixie," and "a shout went up from the impulsive young while the heads of the older were bowed in reverence and their bodies swept by the emotions of memory." After the monument was accepted by a few "choice words" from J.S. Baker, the chorus sang "My Old Kentucky Home," and the ceremony ended.

General Robert E. Lee statue in City Park in Marianna. *Courtesy of the Museum of the Confederacy, Richmond, Virginia.*

The newspaper reporter summed up the account with words that precisely expressed the feelings and thoughts behind the Confederate monument phenomenon across Arkansas and the rest of the South: "In the revolving years that are to come this monument will stand to perpetuate and to memorialize jointly the deeds and daring of the fathers—the love and loyalty of the daughters." The National Register of Historic Places includes the Lee monument.[17]

South of Marianna on the bank of the Mississippi is Helena–West Helena, the site of a Civil War battle on July 4, 1863. The Maple Hill Cemetery on the eastern edge of Crowley's Ridge overlooking the river is the site of three monuments relating to the Confederacy: the General Patrick Cleburne Monument, the monument to the Confederate Soldier and the monument to General Thomas Hindman. About three hundred Confederate soldiers are also buried in the Confederate area established by the Phillips County Memorial Association, and it is on the National Register of Historic Places.

The first monument was built to honor General Patrick Cleburne, who was killed at the Battle of Franklin, Tennessee, on November 30, 1864. He was buried at St. John's Cemetery in Ashwood, Tennessee. In April 1870, the memorial association charged Judge L.H. Mangum and Dr. H.M. Grant to go to Tennessee and return Cleburne's body to Helena, where he had lived before the war. On the day of the reburial in the Confederate portion of Maple Hill Cemetery, all Helena businesses were closed, and a procession over a mile long accompanied his body to the grave site. The Helena Cornet Band led the parade to the cemetery, followed by the Water Witch Fire Department and the hearse, accompanied by fifteen Masons in full regalia who served as the pallbearers. The marshal of the event was behind the hearse, and the ladies of the memorial association followed him in carriages, carrying flowers and wreaths to decorate the Confederate grave sites. The women were followed by a group of young men riding horses and then citizens on foot.

On May 10, 1891, the memorial association dedicated a twenty-five-foot-tall marble shaft to Cleburne's memory, which stands today only a few feet from the larger Confederate soldiers' monument. General George Gordon came to Helena from Memphis to serve as the orator of the day for the Cleburne unveiling. The Chickasaw Guards accompanied Gordon to assist in the memorial service.

The monument to the Confederate soldiers is a tall marble shaft topped by a life-size Confederate soldier statue overlooking the Mississippi River

Confederate major general
Patrick R. Cleburne, circa 1864.
*Courtesy Butler Center for Arkansas
Studies, Arkansas Library Center.*

in the distance. The main part of the monument cost the memorial
association $4,500, and the statue of Italian marble was sculptured in Italy
at a cost of $1,000. It was dedicated on May 25, 1892, and the orator of
the day was Colonel John R. Fellows. The women were proud of the fact
that "every dollar for the monument was paid before it was dedicated."
They had conducted a regionwide campaign to raise the money, including
an appeal in many southern newspapers: "The ladies of Helena are about
to endeavor to raise funds for a Monument to the Confederate dead, to be
erected in the beautiful cemetery at that place, and they will be pleased to
receive any material aid from the friends of the lost cause that they may
feel able to tender," according to a notice in the *Harrison (AR) Times*. They
received not just money in response to their campaign but also plows, carts,
quilts, pigs, sheep, an oil portrait and a bale of cotton. The monument's
inscription reads:

Confederate soldiers monument in Confederate Cemetery in Helena–West Helena. *Courtesy of W. Stuart Towns.*

This Monument Represents
And Embodies Hero Worship
At the Shrine of Patriotism and
Sacrifice, Devotion of the Memory
Of the Lost Cause and Honor to the Soldiers
Known and Unknown Who Rest in Its' Shadow
Unknown Dead
To the Nameless Dead The Fameless Dead
Yet They Made the Fame of Others
This Lofty Shaft is Witness Mute
Of the Love We Bear Beyond Compute
For Our Southland Patriot Brothers

Both the Cleburne and the Confederate monuments are at the top of Crowley's Ridge in the southwest corner of the Maple Hill Cemetery, at the center of the Confederate area that contains the graves of known and unknown Confederate soldiers killed at the Battle of Helena or who died later in the area.

There is also a tall stone shaft at the grave of General Thomas C. Hindman at his family plot close to the entrance of Maple Hill Cemetery. His descendants erected this monument and dedicated it in a private ceremony sometime in the 1930s.[48]

Helena's efforts to raise monuments to the Confederate cause led in the last decade of the nineteenth century to the city being referred to in some publications as "the leading Confederate monument city of that state." The city by the river might still retain that title, as we will see in chapter five, due to its continuing and successful effort to promote its Civil War heritage in the twenty-first century as Arkansas and the South move through the sesquicentennial years.

Continuing south from Helena about 128 miles, Lake Village, on the shore of Lake Chicot, has a Confederate monument on the street positioned between the courthouse lawn and the lake. The soldier is facing the courthouse with his back to the water. The McNeil Marble Company of Marietta, Georgia, crafted it at a cost of $3,000. It was unveiled on October 26, 1910, by the George K. Cracraft and Captain McConnell Chapters of the United Daughters of the Confederacy, and it is dedicated "to the Confederate Soldiers of Chicot County, the record of whose sublime self-sacrifice and undying devotion is the proud heritage of a loyal posterity."

Monument to General Patrick Cleburne at his grave in Confederate Cemetery in Helena–West Helena. *Courtesy of W. Stuart Towns.*

Two years before the unveiling of this monument, George K. Cracraft delivered a speech to the Jacob McConnell Chapter of the United Daughters of the Confederacy on the 100th anniversary of Jefferson Davis's birth. The women were in the midst of their campaign to install the monument, and after discussing the contributions of many residents of the area during the war, he urged the community to memorialize their soldiers in words that echoed across the region at countless other similar events. In a clear call to duty, Cracraft said:

> But have we no other duty to these dead, and is that duty to be postponed? Have we not a splendid manhood left to do greater honor to these heroes and perpetuate their memories? Have we guarded these sacred sepulchres as we should? Have we tired in laying garlands of roses as the only crown of homage? Have we ended our only duty in tears and love? What of the generations to come? No! No! We must say, in earnest silence on the returning anniversary of our greatest hero—
>
> "Without sword or flag, and with soundless tread,
> Once more we will gather our deathless dead,
> Out of their silent graves."
>
> Yes! In such a holy communion with these holy spirits, let us tell them before another year, we have done our final duty. We have builded [sic] a monument to your heroism to endure forever…Do you think there can be higher incentives to honor, virtue, or patriotism, than to look after the needy, and disconsolate…to investigate and record a true history and preserve for coming generations; and last but not least, to build monuments to perpetuate the grandeur of their fame? Let me urge your chapter to build well a grand one for your fathers, brothers, and their comrades, and without delay. Let it grace the grounds of your magnificent temple of justice and may it reflect the thought, that these men fought, bled and died and lost their all for the Justice and the Right.

Chicot County did just that, and the monument graces its lakefront today and is listed on the National Register of Historic Places.[49]

About forty-one miles northeast of Lake Village is Monticello, where the William F. Slemmons Chapter of the United Daughters of the Confederacy dedicated a monument to the Confederate soldiers of Drew County in 1914. It was originally established on the courthouse lawn, but when the old courthouse was demolished and the new one built, the monument was moved to Oakland Cemetery in order to protect it from the construction

Confederate monument in Lake Village, between the Chicot County Courthouse and Lake Chicot. *Courtesy of W. Stuart Towns.*

Confederate soldier monument in Monticello. *Courtesy of W. Stuart Towns.*

work. The shaft has a Confederate soldier statue on the top. On the front are crossed guns and the dedication: "To the Confederate Soldiers of Drew County 1861–1865." The chapter reported $1,013 in its monument fund in 1914, and a historian of Arkansas's monuments estimated that the monument costs were close to $1,500.[50]

Twenty-three miles north of Monticello is Star City, the county seat of Lincoln County. Its Confederate monument is located in a highly visible place on the town square. The J. Martin Meroney Chapter No. 1831 of the United Daughters of the Confederacy unveiled it on October 8, 1928, before "hundreds of Lincoln County citizens" on the courthouse lawn. The memorial is fourteen feet tall and is topped by a white marble sculpture of a soldier resting on his rifle. The statue is a favorite icon of Star City, having gained the nickname "Alex." It was moved from the courthouse lawn in 1962 to the new courthouse but was returned to the town square in 1992. Alex was added to the National Register of Historic Places on April 26, 1996.[51] A small plaque near the memorial reads:

—Erected at Courthouse square in 1928
—Moved to new courthouse in 1962
—Alex returned home in 1992

One of the more unique monuments in Arkansas is at St. Charles, northeast of Dewitt on AR 1. It commemorates the "most destructive shot in the Civil War," the cannon shot that destroyed the Union gunboat USS *Mound City* on June 17, 1862, on the White River at St. Charles. The Union ship was hit by a shot that struck the steam drum and caused an explosion that fatally scalded many of the crew. Some survivors jumped into the river and were targets of the Confederate riflemen. Various sources tally different numbers, but apparently, the crew of 175 men lost at least 105 sailors to the explosion and the sharpshooters.

Years later, the son of William Hickman Harte, one of the sailors who died after the explosion on the *Mound City*, came to St. Charles looking for the grave of his father. He met Judge J.W. Kirkpatrick, who had ministered to the sailor before he died, and he was able to take the son to the spot where his father was buried. Later, the son had the monument erected in the middle of the major street in St. Charles. Another source says the person who commissioned the memorial was a nephew of William H. Harte. The monument is about eighteen feet tall and is a thick, massive structure that bears the inscription:

Confederate monument in Star City in the city square. *Courtesy of W. Stuart Towns.*

"Battle of St. Charles and Explosion of the *Mound City* in White River, Arkansas, in 1862." Engraving from *Harper's Weekly. Courtesy of Butler Center for Arkansas Studies, Arkansas Library.*

In Lasting Memory of William Hickman Harte,
Master, U.S.N.
Born: Limerick, Ireland, 1820. Killed in Action June 17, 1862

There is also a list of 107 names of Federal officers and men killed at the battle inscribed on the monument. It is perhaps the only monument in Arkansas that was erected by a northern individual, and it is one of few in the state that commemorates the dead of both sides. On a panel of the monument is a listing of several Confederates who were killed in the battle. It was dedicated on April 26, 1919, and is on the National Register of Historic Places.[52]

Another unique monument is placed at the junction of Arkansas Highways 8 and 97, just west of New Edinburgh. It is a boulder monument that has two tablets, one on each side of the boulder. As one is driving into New Edinburgh, the tablet on the front is dedicated to Captain Richard Tunstall Banks. On the other side, the tablet discusses the Battle of Marks' Mill, fought in the immediate vicinity of the monument. The monument is placed in a grassy triangle between the junction of the two highways. No record has been found of the date of the dedication or any details about the contributing family or organization. In full, the inscription reads:

Erected to the Memory of
Capt. Richard Tunstall Banks
Serving Under Gen. James Fagan
At the Battle of Marks' Mill
By His Son
A. Burton Banks
His Grandsons
1st Lt. Lawrence Banks
141st Machine Gun BN., 39 Div. World War I
Major Richard Holmes Banks
Army Air Forces, World War I
Robert Theodore Banks
His Great Grandsons
George Banks Collins
Richard Lawrence Collins
Capt. Richard Tunstall Banks Engaged in
Battles of Wilson's Creek, Shiloh, Corinth,
Vicksburg, Marks' Mill, Jenkins Ferry.

Monument in St. Charles. *Courtesy of W. Stuart Towns.*

On the other side is this inscription:

> The Battle of Marks' Mill
> Fought Here on April 25, 1864,
> Was a Complete Confederate Victory.
> Gen. James F. Fagan's Division of Confederate
> Cavalry Surprised and Captured a Union Supply
> Train of 2,000 Men and 240 Wagon Loads of Supplies.
> General Powell Clayton, Union Commander, Narrowly
> Escaped Capture by Flight With Small Detachment.[53]

Pine Bluff's Confederate monument is on the Jefferson County Courthouse lawn and was listed on the National Register of Historic Places on April 26, 1996. It originally was placed on the local high school campus but was later moved to the courthouse. It was dedicated on November 20, 1910, by the David O. Dodd Chapter of the UDC. One of the inscriptions on the monument reads:

> Tribute to David Owen Dodd
> Our Martyr Hero
> Hanged at Little Rock
> As a Spy Jan. 8, 1864,
> Age 17 years.
> He Was Offered life and
> Liberty, But Preferred to
> Die Rather Than Prove
> False to His Trust[54]

About two miles southwest of Pine Bluff is the Sulphur Springs Cemetery monument. It was designed to memorialize Confederate soldiers who died of a smallpox epidemic in the hospital camp at Sulphur Springs. Camp White in Sulphur Springs was a recruiting camp for volunteers from the surrounding area. Units also trained in the area before being deployed east of the Mississippi River. Other troops from Texas and Indian Territory (present-day Oklahoma) were moved into Arkansas to help defend the state, and many were assigned to the Sulphur Springs and Pine Bluff area. After the epidemic claimed an estimated 150 to 175 lives in 1861, most of the troops remaining in the area were transferred to other locations.

Confederate monument unveiling at the Pine Bluff High School campus, July 22, 1910. *Courtesy of the Museum of the Confederacy, Richmond, Virginia.*

The monument was dedicated by the David O. Dodd Chapter of the UDC on October 11, 1912, "in the presence of a large number of people from Pine Bluff and Jefferson County, including Confederate Veterans, sons of veterans and members of the UDC." The orator of the day, T.G. Parham, a Pine Bluff attorney, pointed out:

> *We are assembled here to unveil and to dedicate a monument to the memory of certain Confederate Soldiers who died and whose bodies lie buried upon this spot...Too long have they lain here, nameless in nameless graves, neglected and seemingly forgotten by those who really never can forget... There is something peculiarly sad in the cases of these men. For death came to them, not as soldiers pray that it shall come to them if come it must, where drum beat and trumpets blow the charge and cannons roar, but upon lonely beds of sickness. And God willed that they should bear to their graves with them the scars of smallpox and measles, those, then, two dread diseases, and not the scars of battle. But we know, who stand beside their*

*graves, that they as surely died for the flag they loved as if their bodies had
been riddled by a thousand bullets or torn asunder at the cannon's mouth.*

At the time the document "Confederate Monuments and Markers in
Arkansas" was compiled in 1960, the site had been neglected for years, and
the author wrote, "It is difficult to get close enough to the monument to get
a picture because of the undergrowth." The Dodd Chapter of the UDC
and the Major General Patrick R. Cleburne Camp, No. 1433, SCV, began
to restore the cemetery. In 1996, the two heritage organizations agreed
to preserve and protect the cemetery by installing fencing, flagpoles and
historical markers. Today, the cemetery is well kept and one of the most
interesting and meaningful Civil War sites in Arkansas. There is a small
nature trail around the area.

In addition to the Confederate graves and monument, there is a
monument to Eliza Davis Currie, who was born in 1827 in North Carolina
and who served as a volunteer nurse at the nearby Camp Lee in 1862. She
died of smallpox while caring for ill Confederate soldiers. There is also
an impressive monument to the charter members of the David O. Dodd
Chapter 212 of the United Daughters of the Confederacy, which began on
March 15, 1898. Fifty-two charter members are listed on this monument
dedicated in October 2003. The cemetery was listed on the National Register
of Historic Places on January 19, 2005.[55]

Monuments in Arkansas's Southwest

Camden, about seventy-three miles southwest of Pine Bluff, claims the
honor of erecting the first Confederate monument in Arkansas (some sources
say "west of the Mississippi River") with its May 29, 1886 unveiling of a
memorial in the Greenwood Cemetery—now called Oakland Cemetery.
On Decoration Day the year before, a committee had been formed to place
a monument in memory of the estimated two hundred Confederate soldiers
buried there. According to a report, the unveiling was in "the presence of the
largest crowd ever seen in Camden," with veterans coming from fifty miles
around to participate. The monument cost $1,200. Two members of the
committee had Union ties. Captain J.R. Young had been a Union soldier,
and Mrs. A.A. Tufts was the wife of Captain Tufts, who had also been in
the Union army. The account pointed out that "no others worked more

faithfully than these for its success." The National Register of Historic Places added the Confederate section of the cemetery to its listing in 1996.

The monument is made of Vermont granite and is twenty-five feet tall with a representation of a cannon ball on the top. The inscription on the front of the monument reads:

In Memoriam

1861–1865

Our Confederate Dead[56]

Only a few feet away from this monument is a monument to Hiram L. Grinstead, who had been a colonel in the Thirty-third Arkansas Regiment. He was killed at Jenkins Ferry just after his promotion to brigadier general but before his commission had reached him. The monument is from Italian marble and executed by Morris Bros. of Memphis, from an original design drawn especially for this memorial. It was unveiled on May 6, 1905. Reverend W.F. Evans gave the "solemn invocation," and "an edifying address was delivered by Col. H.S. Bunn in his characteristic manner of thought and humor combined." Each of the Confederate graves in the cemetery was marked with a Confederate flag, and after the unveiling ritual, they were all decorated with fresh flowers.[57]

A third Confederate monument is on the courthouse lawn. It is dedicated to honoring Confederate women. The front of the monument is a figure of a woman holding a flag; just below her feet are the dates 1861–1865 and below that are the words "To Our Confederate Women." On the left side of the monument is this inscription:

Their Inspiration Transformed the Gloom of Defeat Into
The Hope of the Future and Their Memory Shall Not Be
Forgotten Even in the Hours of Peace.

The monument was erected in 1914 and unveiled on May 15, 1915, by the United Confederate Veterans of Hugh McCollum Camp 778; the H.L. Grinstead Chapter, United Daughters of the Confederacy; and Ouachita County. It was listed on the National Register of Historic Places on May 7, 1996.[58]

About ten miles from Camden is the site of the Battle of Poison Springs. Two boulder monuments are located in the Battlefield State Park. One had been unveiled on September 7, 1930, by the H.L. Grinstead UDC

Confederate monument and cemetery plot in Oakland Cemetery in Camden. *Courtesy of W. Stuart Towns.*

Confederate women's monument on the courthouse lawn in Camden. *Courtesy of W. Stuart Towns.*

Chapter 575 of Camden, but it had been uprooted and left in the woods for several years. Another monument placed in 1936 by the Arkansas History Commission had been pushed into a ditch. Both were moved to the entrance of the park and rededicated on April 19, 2008.[59]

Washington served for a time as the war capital of Arkansas, and now it is Historic Washington State Park. One of the earliest monuments in the state was placed here in 1888. It is located on the west side of the Presbyterian Church Cemetery on Highway 4 just north of Washington, where seventy-four Confederate soldiers were buried after they died in this area. In August, the citizens of the town erected a small monument, about twelve feet tall, with a brick base. It was listed on the National Register of Historic Places in 1996. Its inscription reads:

> Erected by our Citizens
> To the memory of our
> Confederate soldiers,
> Who died at this Post during our late Civil War;
> Far from home & kindred.[60]

El Dorado's Confederate monument on the courthouse lawn was designed as a drinking fountain complete with four large columns and a large cap topped with cannon balls and an Italian marble soldier in full stride with his gun on his shoulder. It is about twenty feet tall and fourteen feet square. One source claims that it was the first "memorial fountain" to be built in the South. Its cost was $2,850.

The fountain monument was erected in 1909 and dedicated on March 21, 1910. The speech presenting the memorial to the city was made by the president of the Henry G. Bunn Chapter of the United Daughters of the Confederacy, Mrs. D.W. Thomas, "who paid beautiful tribute to the chivalry of the fallen soldiers." Mr. J.H. Hineman was the principal orator of the day. Mrs. Annie Craig unveiled the monument that had been covered by a Confederate flag twenty by sixty feet in size. The dedication ceremony was attended by seven hundred veterans in uniform. A choir sang Confederate songs, and the local band also played "fine music."

In her description of the monument, Mrs. Thomas wrote, "We daughters feel that we have done all that is left for the wives, daughters and sisters to do to exemplify our love and devotion to the brave souls who fought for our country's honor and our own firesides—that is, to erect a memorial that the memory of the noble sons of our Southland may not fade from the minds

Confederate monument in Presbyterian Cemetery in Old Washington State Park. *Courtesy of W. Stuart Towns.*

of men."[61] These same sentiments were echoed across the state time and time again as monuments were unveiled to honor the Confederate soldier. The National Register of Historic Places added the El Dorado monument in 1996.

Hot Springs has two monuments. One is a monument of granite blocks in the Confederate Lot at Hollywood Cemetery; the other is a classic statue on a column in the heart of downtown. The plot for the burial ground was purchased by David Stone Ryan, who had moved to Hot Springs in 1900. He had been an officer in the Confederate forces from North Carolina and was concerned about where soldiers around his new home could be buried. Before he died in 1907, he had a "goodly number of his comrades laid to rest" in this plot. The Albert Pike United Confederate Veterans camp was disbanded in 1906, and the plot ownership was transferred to the Hot Springs Chapter No. 80 of the UDC to "take charge of, enclose and keep repaired." The members raised money over time for the monument that was dedicated in 1919; it bears the inscription, "Our Confederate Dead." The section is sixty feet by fifty-four feet and contains over thirty Confederate burials.

The UDC members did not stop with this monument and continued a campaign to raise money for a monument to be placed in downtown Hot

Confederate monument at the courthouse in El Dorado. It was originally created as a drinking fountain. *Courtesy of W. Stuart Towns.*

Monument in the Confederate lot of Hollywood Cemetery in Hot Springs. *Courtesy of W. Stuart Towns.*

Springs in an area called at the time Como Square, where Central Avenue, Market Street and Ouachita Avenue converge. The eighteen-foot-tall granite-and-marble monument was made by the McNeel Marble Company of Marietta, Georgia, at a cost of about $5,000. It was erected in November 1933 and dedicated on June 2, 1934.

The small triangle of land where it stands is now called Confederate Memorial Park. The monument was added to the National Register of Historic Places in 1996. In 2002, the UDC and the SCV of Hot Springs undertook a landscaping project to beautify and upgrade Confederate Memorial Park. The two heritage groups asked the community to donate time, help, material and money to the project in hope that "everyone in Hot Springs to be able to say, 'I helped to make this spot beautiful.'"[62]

On Saturday, May 27, 1911, the Harris Flanagin Chapter of the United Daughters of the Confederacy unveiled its monument to the soldiers of the Confederacy on the courthouse lawn at Arkadelphia. The ceremony began at 10:00 a.m. and lasted until late afternoon. The citizens of the town turned out in large numbers, and many came in from the surrounding county, including veterans from the area. The morning program was conducted by Sheriff James H. Abraham and included musical selections, prayers and speeches. One of the highlights was an oration by a young man, Farrar Newberry, which was described as "a stirring and patriotic oration in which he eulogized the soldiers of the Confederacy in the highest terms and praised the Confederate ladies for their grand achievement." After a recess for lunch, Captain Blake's band provided "inspiring music for the occasion," followed by more speeches and "one of the most impressive numbers on the program, the singing of 'Dixie' by the Daughters of the Confederacy, those loyal hearts whose devotion to their beloved southland never wanes." After a stirring speech by Professor J.H. Hinemon, the veterans assembled at the base of the monument, and Mrs. Butler and Mr. Abraham unveiled the monument to a "mighty shout" from the audience. The ceremonies concluded with the serving of "cooling refreshments without charge" to the veterans by a "bevy of beautiful young ladies, each wearing a sash of patriotic colors." Cadets from Ouachita College presented a "most creditable exhibition drill."

As the women of the UDC were soon to find out, their work had just begun. A letter in the *Southern Standard* newspaper of Arkadelphia made clear the task ahead of them as the president of the organization wrote:

Confederate soldier statue in Confederate Memorial Park in Hot Springs. *Courtesy of W. Stuart Towns.*

Confederate monument in Arkadelphia on the Clark County Courthouse lawn. *Courtesy of W. Stuart Towns.*

The Harris Flanagin chapter of the UDC have had a monument erected on the court house grounds in honor of all the soldiers who went from this and adjoining counties, to fight in the Confederate Army.

Their faith in the sons, daughters, grandsons, and granddaughters of the faithful men who suffered through that awful period made them willing to take the responsibility of ordering the monument with almost no money in the treasury, feeling sure that the loyal sons and daughters of the South would come to their assistance and help raise the money. We must raise $60 per month for two years, to get it paid for in the time allowed.

This is no child's task. It will take much work on the part of all the members of the UDC and the hearty co-operating of every man, woman, and child in a radius of thirty miles to accomplish it. If you had a male relative in the Confederate Army it is to honor him that we have attempted this gigantic work. We feel that we were right in doing it, for we feel that our children need just such inspiration to noble, heroic living as this monument will rouse in their hearts.

When you come to town bring your children to see the monument, have them memorize the inscriptions and teach them to honor their forefathers as they should. Miss Etta Thomas is our treasurer; if you will help us send your contributions to her.

Yours for a return to the noble principles of our fathers.

Mrs. J.S. Cargile
Pres. Harris Flanagin Chapter UDC

Apparently, not a lot of contributions rolled in to Miss Thomas. A series of articles in the local newspaper over the next four years illustrated the plight of the UDC. On June 29, 1911, another appeal went out and the ladies promised to publish monthly the names of "those who help us in the work." The list in the paper that day included gifts of $5.00, $3.50, fifteen gifts of $1.00 each and four contributions of $0.50. The ultimate goal was $1,500. The group sponsored a play, *A Woman's Honor*, at the Gresham Theatre, which was well received but produced only $20.80 for the monument fund. A bazaar was held, and the UDC members were asked to each produce something that could be sold—preserves, pickles, jellies, canned fruits or "anything that can be worn, eaten, or used in a home, will be acceptable." The goal of the bazaar was to raise $900.00. Apparently, the goal was not reached, as on May 7, 1914, the chapter sent out an appeal "over the state" requesting $1.00 contributions; at this point, the debt to the monument company was one year overdue. Finally, in November 1915, the women went to the Clark County Levying Court with an appeal to pay the remainder in full. Mrs. L.S. Butler made a heartrending, passionate appeal to the justices of the peace. Among other things, Mrs. Butler said:

> *In nearly every battle of the war some Clark county boy lost his life, and his bones, washed from shallow graves by floods or disinterred by wild beasts, repose as souvenirs of that unequal struggle amid sabre and musket, cannon ball and grapeshot, shrapnel and Minnie ball, garnered from every battle field of the South. Perhaps, gentlemen, you have some loved one you would like to have remembered. Perhaps a friend, a father or a brother is sleeping his last sleep at Shiloh or Franklin, at Chickamauga or Corinth. Perhaps Virginia claims his blood to enrich her soil and he sleeps in the trenches at Manassas or Fredericksburg, at Chancellorsville with Stonewall Jackson or in the crater at Petersburg; or, defending his own state, he fell at Pea Ridge or Poison Springs, at Mark's Mill [sic] or Jenkins' Ferry. Wherever he may have fallen his memory calls to you for some token of remembrance for his great sacrifice in defending Clark county soil.*

Although five voted against it, the measure passed, and the county appropriated $665 to pay off the monument. A last notice, "Expresses Thanks to All," appeared in the local newspaper on December 16, 1915: "The Harris Flanagin Chapter, UDC extends to all the friends who have assisted them in any way in paying the debt on the Confederate monument… This debt has been a night mare to the chapter for five years and the relief they feel cannot be expressed in words."

There was another major issue with the monument when a tornado ripped through Arkadelphia on March 1, 1997, badly damaging the statue and requiring significant repairs. The UDC created a fund for the repairs and also earmarked the fund to deal with similar events as they occurred. Repairs were completed, and the monument was rededicated on Saturday, October 12, 2002. Pamela Trammell, president of the Arkansas Division of the UDC, told the audience at the ceremony: "It's our history. Without our history, we lose so much. If our kids are going to remember, we've got to put them back up." The monument was placed on the National Register of Historic Places on May 3, 1996. [63]

Monuments in Arkansas's Northwest

Moving into the northwest corner of the state, one might expect to find fewer Confederate memorials, as the northern regions of Arkansas saw more Union sentiment than southern Arkansas. But we find today several more monuments and memorials than in the northeast area of the state, and even more than the southeast corner.

Starting in Russellville, we find one of the most unique memorials, the Confederate Mothers Memorial Park, a rustic park at the summit of the hills around Russellville. It is located at the intersection of Skyline Drive (Highway 326) and South Glenwood Avenue. Twenty acres belonging to Judge and Mrs. Robert B. Wilson were donated to the United Daughters of the Confederacy in Russellville, under the condition that it "be preserved as a park and playground for children, as a memorial to them of the bravery of Southern womanhood." Plans were made to make the area a bird sanctuary, and local boys built birdhouses for that purpose. Roads and a pavilion were constructed, and within a short time, the park became "a place where the citizens [drove] to sit under the shelter of the pines, and talk over the old days of sacrifice and hardship, and none can visit the spot without being impressed."

An account of the park in a 1923 issue of *Confederate Veteran* magazine introduced an early version of historical tourism:

> *Many tourists from all parts of the country pass through Russellville for it lies at the gateway where hill and valley meet, and through the little city one must go to visit the great Diamond Cave in the mountains of an adjoining county. The scenery is beautiful around the little town; on one side a prairie; on the north, foothills of the Ozarks, back of the twinkling lights of a State District Agricultural College; south of Russellville lies the Arkansas River, flanked on either bank by bold bluffs, one called Dardanelle Rock, noted for its legends...Across the river between Dardanelle and Russellville runs the longest pontoon bridge in the world, built some fifty years ago...Back of Dardanelle, rising majestically above the surrounding country, is Mount Nebo, around whose head the clouds gather in great billows on foggy mornings.*

There is a monument in the park "dedicated to the happiness of the children of our united county." The single word "Mother" is inscribed on the front below the furled flag and laurel wreath on the top of the shaft. Two

Confederate Mothers Park in Russellville. *Courtesy of W. Stuart Towns.*

Boulder monument in Confederate Mothers Park in Russellville. *Courtesy of W. Stuart Towns.*

rock columns grace the entrance to the park, and they were dedicated on June 12, 1924. Each column bears inscriptions honoring the Ben T. Embry Camp of the Sons of Confederate Veterans and the John R. Homer Scott Chapter of the United Daughters of the Confederacy.

The park is part of the Russellville park system and is maintained by the Recreation and Parks Department, with help from the River Valley Living History Association. It was added to the National Register of Historic Places in 1996.[64]

Just across the Arkansas River from the Confederate Mothers Park is a Confederate soldier statue on the Yell County Courthouse lawn in Dardanelle. The monument was erected by the United Daughters of the Confederacy in 1921. The Joe Wheeler Chapter boasted of the fact that it had raised the $1,760 for the monument without any outside help.

The unveiling and dedication ceremony on June 3 was "a most impressive event and one that will never be forgotten by those in attendance, from the oldest white-haired, tottering old veteran who marched in the parade to the youngest of the sweet little flower girls who bedecked the base of the handsome memorial with flowers." The program was held in the First Presbyterian Church, followed by a parade to the monument and the presentation of the monument to the city by Mrs. P.G. Blevins and acceptance by county judge T.E. Wilson and Mayor Reece Batson. After the ceremony, the thirty-three veterans, the UDC and invited guests were served "a sumptuous dinner" at Miller's Hall.

When the monument was first dedicated, it was located between two banks in downtown Dardanelle, but after a bridge was built over the river in 1930, the monument was moved to its current location so that "all who crossed the bridge would find themselves face to face with the image in marble of the greatest soldier in the world—the Confederate soldier." It was placed on the National Register of Historic Places in 1996.[65]

Back on the north side of the Arkansas River, the city of Clarksville is the location of a Confederate monument, this one in a local cemetery. There were about 170 unknown Confederate soldiers buried in the cemetery owned by the Methodist Episcopal Church, South. The church's board of trustees decided to reinter them in one small square plot. A monument was erected in the middle of that plot. Citizens of Clarksville carried out this process in 1891, before either the UDC or UCV were formed. By 1908, the Felix I. Batson Chapter of the UDC was established, and they placed small, unlettered headstones of marble at each grave. According to the minutes of this chapter, the monument was in place by 1902. It is on the National Register of Historic Places.[66]

Confederate soldiers monument in Dardanelle. *Courtesy of W. Stuart Towns.*

Confederate monument in Oakland Cemetery in Clarksville. *Courtesy of W. Stuart Towns.*

Driving west on I-40, the Franklin County Courthouse lawn in Ozark is the location of a small monument. As the Arkansas River divides the county, the difficulty crossing the river in the 1800s led to creating a second county seat at Charleston before the turn of the century. The monument on the Ozark courthouse grounds memorializes a Confederate officer killed in fighting just north of town.[67]

Crossing the Arkansas River again, Charleston is our next stop, where there is a tablet monument on the courthouse lawn. It was placed by the Pat Cleburne Camp of the United Confederate Veterans. The inscription reads:

In God We Trust
Honoring our Confederate
Veterans
1861----------1865
Pat Cleburne Camp No. 191[68]

Continuing west on Arkansas Highway 22, Fort Smith is the next location of Confederate memorials. Incidentally, Highway 22 is part of the Jefferson Davis Highway sponsored by the United Daughters of the Confederacy. In 1835, Lieutenant Jefferson Davis was in charge of surveying the road from Dardanelle to Fort Smith, which was a major outpost of the U.S. Army at that time, and the road was used to expedite the infamous Indian removal process. The Arkansas General Assembly passed Bill No. 66 on January 30, 1925, that authorized the naming of the highway. The Arkansas Division of the UDC placed stone and bronze markers at the Yell County Courthouse and on the highway right of way in Dardanelle and Fort Smith.

There are four monuments regarding the Confederacy in Fort Smith. The most notable is the statue on the Sebastian County Courthouse lawn. About a decade after the war's end, a sandstone marker was placed in the Fort Smith National Cemetery in honor of 2 Confederate generals who had died in battle, General A.E. Steen at Prairie Grove and General James McIntosh at Pea Ridge. On January 11, 1898, that monument was destroyed in a tornado, and the federal government replaced the shaft with a simple marker with the generals' names and "The Unknown Confederate Dead" inscribed on it. There were 318 Confederate soldiers who were buried in the area around the 2 generals' graves and the monument. Many in Fort Smith thought that was an inadequate memorial, and later that year, the Varina Jefferson Davis Chapter of the UDC was organized to "fulfill the duties of sacred charity toward monument to our dead."

Over the next five years, the Daughters raised $2,332.39 by holding "teas, dances, suppers, booths at street fairs and various entertainments." The plans were to install it in the National Cemetery to replace the much smaller memorial to the generals. But the quartermaster general of the army and secretary of the army, Elihu Root, decided that it could not be placed in the cemetery due to symbols such as the crossed Confederate flags, the statue of the Confederate Soldier and especially the words "LEST WE FORGET" engraved on the base. Local newspapers and organizations strongly opposed the "suggested modifications," and in January 1903, the city council gave permission to place the monument on the courthouse grounds.

On September 10, 1903, at 2:00 p.m., the monument was unveiled to a large audience, Confederate veterans in uniform and a marching band. Among other speakers on the program, Senator James H. Berry was the featured orator of the day. Mr. Joseph M. Hill, the youngest son of Confederate general Daniel H. Hill, presented the monument to the Varina Jefferson Davis Chapter.[69] It was placed on the National Register of Historic Places in 1996.

One of the most unique Confederate sculptures is a private tombstone in the Oak Cemetery at 1401 South Greenwood in Fort Smith. It is at the burial site of Captain James E. Reynolds and depicts a wounded Captain Reynolds being helped from the battlefield at New Hope, Georgia, by two teenage girls. Reynolds died on June 26, 1920.

A third Confederate memorial is in the Forest Park Cemetery at 5001 Midland Boulevard in Fort Smith and is a small tablet marker that reads, "Confederate Soldiers Rest in This Circle." It is accompanied by a flagpole with a Confederate flag.

The final memorial in Fort Smith is the Jefferson Davis Memorial that highlights the Jefferson Davis Highway that became Arkansas Highway 22. The monument is by the side of the highway. It was erected by the Varina Jefferson Davis Chapter of the United Daughters of the Confederacy in 1937.[70]

A short distance from Fort Smith across the Arkansas River is Van Buren, where there is a monument on the courthouse lawn. It had originally been placed in the Fairview Cemetery in 1899, where some 433 unknown Confederate soldiers were buried. The Mary Lee Chapter of the United Daughters of the Confederacy was formed in Van Buren on March 19, 1898, with one of its goals to erect a monument "to the memory of their fallen heroes, who had been sleeping a third of a century, their graves unmarked save by the pines that grew into sentinel-like forms about their unnamed graves." Most of the burials were soldiers from Missouri, Arkansas, Texas,

Confederate soldier monument in Fort Smith on the courthouse lawn. *Courtesy of W. Stuart Towns.*

Louisiana and the Indian Territory who had died in a hospital in Van Buren after the battles of Wilson's Creek, Pea Ridge or Prairie Grove.

The women of Van Buren "worked faithfully for this attainment" and accomplished the fundraising in about a year under the "unceasing effort" of Miss Frances M. Scott, "the hardest worker for the cause in the State." An article in the *Confederate Veteran* announcing her death referred to her work and said, "This is largely her monument." The memorial is made from Italian marble and is twenty-one feet high, with a life-size figure of a Confederate soldier on the top. The inscription on the base is:

1899.
1861. C.S.A. 1865.
Erected by the
Mary Lee Chapter
United Daughters of the
Confederacy.

Above the inscription are two crossed Confederate flags, and above them are the words:

Furled, but not forgotten.

On the opposite side is inscribed:

Captain A. Churchill Clarke
Battery A. Missouri.
Killed at Elkhorn, March 6, 1862
Aged 20 Years.

On one side is the great seal of the Confederacy, and on the other side are the Confederate names and the dates of the three battles in which these soldiers died: Oak Hill, August 10, 1861; Elkhorn, March 6, 1862; Prairie Grove, December 7, 1862.

The monument was moved to the courthouse lawn and rededicated on August 4, 1906, and was named to the National Register of Historic Places in 1996.[71]

The Fayetteville Confederate Cemetery is home to one of the finest monuments in the state. As we discussed in chapter two, the Southern Memorial Association of Washington County built the cemetery, maintains it even today, still honors the Confederate soldiers buried there with an annual Memorial Day commemoration and was responsible for erecting the monument in the center of the cemetery.

The SMA met on October 13, 1896, to discuss the sixteen designs for the monument that had been submitted. They selected the plans of the F.H. Venn Company of Memphis, Tennessee. The total amount for the monument had not been completely raised by that time, so through the fall and winter, the women continued to raise money. On December 7, the anniversary of the Battle of Prairie Grove, they sponsored a "literary and musical entertainment," the proceeds of which were to go to the monument fund. A "Grand Song Tournament or Cantata" was staged and led by Mrs. Seth E. Meek. A card and Parcheesi party was held at the Van Winkle Hotel, which cost participants twenty-five cents, to go to the fund. A lecture and reading by Booth Lowry of Mississippi was held on the coldest night of the year in Wood's Opera House and drew only "a few faithful."

Another idea for the fundraising was apparently more successful. Members and friends of the SMA sent out small booklets each with

Confederate soldier monument in Van Buren on the courthouse lawn. *Courtesy of W. Stuart Towns.*

pockets for ten dimes. A historian of the association recounted that she was "of errand age" at that time and could recall distributing and collecting some of these cards. The booklets were "filled by willing hands and freighted with good wishes of encouragement" from people from the four states represented by the monument—Arkansas, Texas, Louisiana and Missouri—as well as donors from "all over the country." By February 16, 1897, Mrs. Lizzie Pollard, the president of the SMA, said all but $511 had been raised for the monument.

The cornerstone was dedicated on May 1, 1897, when a "good-sized crowd" gathered for the ceremony. The cornerstone was filled with a list of the soldiers buried in the cemetery, a list of Arkansas Industrial University students who had donated to the fund and the first silver dollar contributed to the monument. The monument arrived shortly afterward, and when it reached the Frisco railroad station, Mr. A.M. Byrnes, a "local contractor and a public-spirited citizen, happened to be at the depot. He immediately

Monument in the Fayetteville Confederate Cemetery. *Courtesy of W. Stuart Towns.*

got a crew busy hauling the tall shaft up the hill to the cemetery, where he personally supervised the placing of the monument."

The unveiling was set for the twenty-fifth anniversary of the founding of the Southern Memorial Association, June 10, 1897, and it drew the "largest crowd ever assembled, before or since, at the Confederate Cemetery." One estimate had the crowd size at ten thousand onlookers. The Arkansas Industrial University cadets marched up the hill in a body, and the AIU band and the Fort Smith Drum Corps provided the music for the decoration of the graves and the dedication ritual. J. Vol Walker delivered the oration of the day, in which he said, "We stand here in peace today, with respect and without reproach for the Union soldier, with love and without apology for the Confederate, to do honor to the memory of our dead." Mrs. Pollard unveiled the monument and then "made a talk of revealing content and inspiring appeal." The memorial is a granite shaft topped by a bronze statue of a Confederate soldier.[72]

Many of the dead in the Fayetteville Confederate Cemetery were killed at the Battle of Prairie Grove, about nine miles southwest of Fayetteville on U.S. Highway 62. The battleground is now a state park, but the memorializing of the battle and the Confederates who fought there began in 1908, when the Prairie Grove Chapter of the United Daughters of the Confederacy bought 9 acres at the south edge of the battle site. By the twenty-first century, the park included 838 acres of the 3,000-acre battlefield. Prairie Grove was a major battle where 2,700 lost their lives.

The UDC moved the stone chimney of the nearby Rhea's Mill to the site, built a rock wall around that area and dedicated it to the soldiers who had fought there on December 7, 1862. The chimney is fifty-five feet tall, eight feet square at the base and four feet square at the top. It is made of seven hundred Ozark stones. The wall is considered "history in stone," according to a historian of the site, as it was constructed with stones from historic structures all over Washington County, such as stagecoach stations, pioneer homes, post offices, churches, schools and other buildings.

There are several monuments in the area around the park headquarters. The chimney is one, and the two rock pillars at the entrance to the park were also dedicated to warriors. The left pillar reads:

Dedicated
To The
Soldiers
of
1861–1865   1917–1918

Dedication of Battle Monument

at PRAIRIE GROVE, ARKANSAS

FRIDAY, DECEMBER 7, 1956

on the 94th anniversary of the battle.

2:30 o'clock   Battlefield Park*

Program

DR. H. E. BUCHANAN, presiding

Music

Invocation .... Rev. Stanley Bright

Introduction of Trustees and Officers of Battlefield Memorial Foundation

"The Battle of Prairie Grove" .... Dr. Robert R. Logan

"The Story of the Park" .... Mrs. J. C. Parks

Presentation of Park Deed .... Mrs. Lincoln Maupin, president
            and members of the United Daughters of the Confederacy

"Rhea's Mill" .... Admiral Powell Rhea, USN Ret.

"The Monument" .... Dr. Calvin Bain

Gift of Monument to Memorial Foundation
                    ...... Mr. and Mrs. George C. Mennecke, Sr.

"Plans for Development":

        The Story .... Dr. Fred McCuistion

        The Plans .... Prof. John Williams

"Meaning of Historic Restoration to Arkansas" .... Ted R. Worley

Introduction of descendants of men who fought in the battle

Song, "God Bless America" .... Miss Myrtilla Dorman

Benediction .... Rev. R. E. L. Bearden

        *In the event of bad weather, the program will be given in the
                    Auditorium of the Methodist Church

Program for the Prairie Grove monument dedication on December 7, 1956.
Courtesy Old State House Museum Collection.

On the right pillar is inscribed:

Erected
By The
Daughters
Of
Confederacy   1924

Another monument is the State Park Museum and Headquarters building. It was created by a donation from Confederate general Thomas Hindman's son, Biscoe Hindman, who left $100,000 in his will to the State of Arkansas for the memorial to be built at Prairie Grove. It was completed and dedicated on May 23, 1965.[73]

At Pea Ridge National Military Park north of Rogers on U.S. 62 and near the Missouri state line, there are two Civil War monuments. The 4,210-acre park was established in 1960, after the State of Arkansas had purchased the land through the 1957 general assembly's Act 192 and donated the land to the National Park Service. Pea Ridge, sometimes called Elkhorn Tavern, was a significant and hard-fought battle that preserved Missouri for the Union and ended serious resistance to Union control of northern Arkansas and southern Missouri.

The first monument erected in the battlefield area was built in 1887 by citizens of Benton County to memorialize the Confederates who had died at Pea Ridge, including Generals Ben McCulloch of Texas, W.Y. Slack of Missouri and James McIntosh from Arkansas. The name of each of the generals is placed on each of the three sides of the monument, and on the fourth is engraved, "The brave Confederate dead, who fell on this field March 7 and 8, 1862." At the dedication ceremony on September 1, Congressman S.W. Peel welcomed the audience, which included both Confederate and Union veterans from the area. One of the several speakers on the program that day noted this fact as he said, "The white dove seemed to spread her wings alike over all. And harmony reigned supreme as men from both armies honored the dead at this battlefield." The orator of the day was former Texas governor Lubbock, who praised both the "Blue and the Grey" for their bravery and urged the audience to "stand by the old constitution as it now is, and be a loyal and conservative people."

The second monument was established by both Union and Confederate veterans in September 1889 and is known as the "Reunited Soldiery Monument." The monument is about seventeen feet tall and is topped

Confederate monument in Pea Ridge National Battlefield Park. *Courtesy of W. Stuart Towns.*

Blue-Gray Monument in Pea Ridge National Battlefield Park. *Courtesy of W. Stuart Towns.*

Close-up of engraving on the Blue-Gray Monument in Pea Ridge National Battlefield Park. *Courtesy of W. Stuart Towns.*

with an angel of peace made from Italian marble. The angel is looking down at the clasped hands of the Blue and Gray soldiers who are at peace. Even though the weather was bad, an estimated seven thousand persons attended the reunion of the Blue and Gray and the monument dedication just a few feet away from the Confederate monument and adjacent to Elkhorn Tavern.[74]

The city of Bentonville, to the west of Pea Ridge, has a Confederate monument in the beautiful and well-maintained city square in the heart of town. The monument was unveiled on August 8, 1908. Special cars on trains from Fort Smith, Fayetteville and Missouri arrived in Bentonville carrying many celebrants. The commemoration began with a band concert on the lawn of the courthouse followed by an informal parade to Park Springs, where there was a typical program of music and speeches. Hugh A. Dinsmore was the main speaker for this part of the program. A lunch break followed, and "a sumptuous old-fashioned basket dinner was served with Park Spring water—cold, clear, and inviting and the only beverage. Everybody was invited."

At 1:30 that afternoon, the parade started. It featured a "beautiful white float that looked like a moving bank of red and white roses." Its cargo was "fourteen pretty girls in white representing the seceded states." They were followed by several "beautifully decorated carriages" and a rose-covered float bearing members of the Southern Memorial Association and the Sterling Price UDC Chapter. Behind them were "many decorated carriages," the Sons of Confederacy and citizens. At the city square, the unveiling took place with the usual music and speeches. Reverend R.E.L. Bearden gave the invocation. An account of the event said of the speeches: "Major Clifton R. Breckenridge of Fort Smith was the able and eloquent orator for the occasion. Hugh A. Dinsmore also made a splendid speech." The young ladies who had represented the Confederate states pulled the cords holding the red-and-white veil, and it fell from the statue. A local citizen, A.J. Bates, who had been a private in General Shelby's Missouri Brigade, donated $1,000 for the monument, and the local James H. Berry Chapter, UDC, raised the balance of the $2,500 the monument cost. The granite statue was made by the Charles Scott Company of Barre, Vermont, and is listed on the National Register of Historic Places.[75]

MONUMENTS IN CENTRAL ARKANSAS

As might be thought, the Little Rock and surrounding area has a high concentration of monuments and memorials to the Confederacy. The concentration of population and better economic conditions in the urban area are probably contributing factors, but whatever the case, the area has some of the finest sites to visit.

First, let's look at the four that are not far outside Pulaski County. The Camp Nelson Cemetery near Cabot has a monument in the center of the burial ground for 428 Texas Confederates who died of a measles epidemic while camped in the area in 1862. T.J. Young, the adjutant of the James Adams Camp, No. 1036, attempted to raise the funds for the cemetery but was not immediately successful. After making an appeal to the Arkansas General Assembly, the 1905 legislature appropriated $1,000 to the project. The cemetery was completed and the monument dedicated on October 4, 1906. Its shaft is made from Batesville marble and is about twelve feet tall. At the dedication, Dr. John A. Martin, "a gallant Confederate soldier," made the dedication speech, while Miss Mabel Vess, granddaughter of veteran J.M.

Gately, who donated the ground for the cemetery, and Miss Issie Mulkey, daughter of another veteran, unveiled the monument. After several speeches by other community leaders, 27 Confederate veterans marched around the monument, and each placed a piece of cedar on the base as "a token of love for their unknown comrades."[76]

Four years after the original dedication of the Camp Nelson cemetery and monument, Lonoke County erected its second memorial to the Confederate soldier. The monument of Georgia marble was erected by the T.C. Hindman Chapter of the UDC. The ladies raised about $1,000 of the $1,500 cost, and the balance was provided by the Quorum Court of Lonoke County. The cornerstone was laid in June 1910 and contained memorabilia—such as several bills of Confederate money, pictures of various veterans, cards and mementos and the rosters of the James McIntosh UCV Camp and the T.C. Hindman UDC Chapter—donated by citizens. The dedication took place on October 20, 1910, and featured the speech of Congressman Joe T. Robinson of Lonoke, who was in the midst of a successful campaign for governor. The monument is twenty-five feet high and topped with a statue of a Confederate soldier. An inscription drives home the purpose of the monument: "Lonoke County commends the faithfulness of her sons to future generations." The monument is on the county courthouse lawn and is listed on the National Register of Historic Places.[77]

Conway's Robert E. Lee Chapter of the UDC dedicated its monument on October 18, 1925, on the Faulkner County Courthouse lawn. It cost around $1,500 and is about eighteen feet tall, topped with a pyramid. Its main inscription reads:

> Dedicated To The Memory
> Of Our Confederate Soldiers
> The Bravest Of The Brave

The monument is located at the corner of Robinson Avenue and Center Street and was listed on the National Register of Historic Places on April 26, 1996.[78]

Moving to the Little Rock area, the first site is the Little Rock National Cemetery at 2523 Confederate Boulevard, just east of I-30, exit 139. It was established on April 9, 1868, and was used to bury Union soldiers who died in Arkansas. In 1884, an adjoining section of land became an eleven-acre Confederate cemetery, and in 1934, the two were combined and the wall between them torn down. Confederate and Union burials were, however, kept separate.

Confederate monument in Conway on the courthouse lawn. *Courtesy of W. Stuart Towns.*

Confederate veterans monument from 1884 in the Confederate Section of Little Rock National Cemetery. *Courtesy of W. Stuart Towns.*

There are three notable sites in the Confederate section. The first one established is the marble monument placed in 1884 by the Trustees of the Mount Holly Cemetery when the Confederate cemetery was created. The inscription on this short monument reads: "Here Lies the Remains of 640 Confederate Soldiers from Arkansas, Missouri, Texas and Louisiana Who Died in the Years 1861, 1862, and 1863. They Were Buried in Mt. Holly Cemetery and Were Removed to This Spot in the Year 1884."

The second memorial constructed is the gray brick and tile-roofed speaker's stand that was erected in 1907 for $608. There is a marble slab on one side that is inscribed:

> Stoop, Angels, higher from the skies
> There is no holier spot of ground
> Than where defeated valor lies
> By Mourning beauty crowned.
> Erected by Memorial Chapter,
> United Daughters of the Confederacy

Confederate monument in Little Rock National Cemetery. *Courtesy of W. Stuart Towns.*

The third monument in the cemetery is a tall obelisk erected for $650 in 1913 by the UDC. It is dedicated, "In memory of the nine hundred Confederate soldiers buried within this enclosure, most of whom died in the hospitals in Little Rock in 1863." It was dedicated on May 11, 1913, and is listed on the National Register of Historic Places.[79]

Not far from the Confederate Section of the Little Rock National Cemetery on the west side of I-30 is MacArthur Park, site of the Arsenal Building, now the MacArthur Museum of Arkansas Military History, and three Confederate memorial locations. David O. Dodd, the "boy hero" of the Confederacy, is memorialized with a boulder type of monument identifying the place where he was executed for spying. The actual site was several hundred yards to the east, and the monument was originally erected there. Due to construction of the interstate highway, it was moved in the 1960s to its present location by the parking lot to the side of the MacArthur Museum. The inscription reads:

In Memory of
David O. Dodd
The Boy Hero of the Confederacy
This Marks the Spot of His Execution
Jan. 8, 1864
Erected by the Memorial Chapter
U.D.C.
1926

In that same area, near the MacArthur Museum, there is a concrete bench placed by the Children of the Confederacy chapter in October 1936 "in memory of the youth of the State of Arkansas who gave their loyal service to the Cause of the Confederacy in the War 1861–1865."

In front of the Arsenal Building there is an outstanding monument that was dedicated at the time of the 1911 United Confederate Veterans' national reunion in Little Rock. It is a memorial to the Capital Guards, a Little Rock militia unit that was involved in the takeover of the arsenal in February 1861 in one of the first actions of the Civil War. The unit later served as Company A of the Sixth Arkansas Infantry and was part of General Patrick Cleburne's division. The pedestal is a tall white granite shaft topped with a bronze Confederate soldier statue. Its dedication was an important part of the UCV reunion on May 17, 1911. One of the monument's inscriptions quotes a statement from General Hardee's report after the battle of Franklin, Tennessee, in which General Cleburne was killed: "When his division

Unveiling of the Capitol Guard Monument in Little Rock in 1911. *Courtesy of the UALR Center for Arkansas History and Culture.*

defended, no odds could break its lines; when it attacked, no numbers resisted its onslaught."[80]

There is a monument to David O. Dodd in the Mount Holly Cemetery on Broadway Street, where he was buried. It is a plain marble shaft with the words, "David Owen Dodd, the boy hero of Arkansas, Born November the 10th, 1846, died January 8, 1864." The Sons of Confederate Veterans commemorate his death each January with reenactors firing three volleys, speakers and appropriate music. In 1998, the speaker was former governor Sid McMath, who, at age eighty-five, recalled helping to feed old veterans at one of their conventions in Little Rock.[81]

Little Rock can claim another David O. Dodd memorial, the monument that is on the east side of the Old State House Museum grounds. This monument is inscribed with paragraphs describing his story and this engraved eulogy to the young man:

> *Aye, such was the love of the boy for his southland*
> *Such his endurance, his courage, his pride,*
> *That e'er he'd betray his own beloved band*
> *He sacrificed all, and silently died.*

David O. Dodd Monument at the Old State House Museum in Little Rock. *Courtesy of W. Stuart Towns.*

The idea for the monument came from two high school students in Little Rock who became interested in Dodd as they were studying American heroes in their history class. As adults, Mrs. Kathleen Kavanaugh and Mrs. P.J. Rice continued their interest and enlisted the UCV, the UDC and the SCV organizations for the fundraising efforts. The inscriptions were written by the president of the Arkansas Division UDC, Mrs. George B. Gill. The dedication address was presented by Governor McRae. A unique part of the ceremony was the reading of a letter from two of Dodd's sisters, Mrs. Leonora Dodd Richmond and Mrs. Senora Dodd Booth, of Washington, D.C., expressing gratitude for the monument to their brother. It was unveiled on November 10, 1923.[82]

Another Little Rock–area monument to Dodd is on the campus of the David O. Dodd School, on Stagecoach Road. It was erected by the David O. Dodd Chapter of the UDC of Pine Bluff, Arkansas, and notes that this was the place where he was captured by Union troops on December 31, 1863. An inscription reads: "He died to save—we live to serve."[83]

Another boulder monument is just a few yards west of the Dodd School at 6915 Stagecoach Road, which memorializes the "Last Stand" of the Confederates in Little Rock. It is near the historic 10 Mile House on Arkansas

Highway 5, also called Stagecoach Road, and was erected by the General T.J. Churchill Chapter of the UDC on October 15, 1929. The 10 Mile House was built between 1825 and 1836 and is perhaps "the most historically significant home in Arkansas history," according to Kay Tatum, president of the General T.J. Churchill Chapter. It is about one-quarter mile east of the I-430 and Stagecoach Road exit. The inscription on the boulder reads:

Last Stand Made
By Confederates
September 11, 1863
After the fall of
Little Rock[84]

The Churchill Chapter and the Arkansas Division of the UDC and the Arkansas Division of the SCV held a rededication of this monument on September 14, 2013.

While not a traditional monument or marker, I would be remiss in not mentioning another memorial to David O. Dodd in the Little Rock area: the David O. Dodd Window in the MacArthur Museum of Arkansas Military History in the Old Arsenal Building at MacArthur Park. It was originally placed in the Arkansas Room of the White House of the Confederacy Museum in Richmond, Virginia, on Tuesday, November 7, 1911, after it had been donated to the museum by the Arkansas Division of the UDC. At some unknown point later, the window was taken down and put into storage. In the late 1980s, it was loaned to the Arkansas Museum of Science and History, now the Museum of Arkansas Military History. It was unveiled in a ceremony on Saturday, February 10, 1990. The Arkansas Division of the Sons of Confederate Veterans participated in the unveiling.[85]

There are two monuments to Arkansas's Confederate women in Little Rock. The smaller is a granite boulder with a tablet that is located on the grounds of the Old State House Museum. The J.M. Keller Chapter, United Daughters of the Confederacy, erected this small monument on November 9, 1910.[86]

The major monument to the women of the state is located on the southeast corner of the state capitol grounds. This memorial is the second monument to the women of the Confederacy in the South. The first one was dedicated in South Carolina in 1912. The idea of honoring the women with impressive monuments grew out of a committee of the United Confederate Veterans established in the late 1890s that worked to erect a monument to the women in every southern state. In 1906, the

Arkansas Division began to raise money using the sale of a book by J.M. Lucey that was a collection of stories and poems from and about Arkansas women. *Confederate Women of Arkansas* sold for $0.50 cents in paperback and $1.00 in cloth cover and eventually earned $500 for the monument fund. The veterans went to the state legislature and received a $10,000 appropriation in 1911 that considerably speeded up the process.

The sculptor was a widely known Swiss artist, J. Otto Schweizer. He was selected by a committee that heard presentations from many of the twenty-eight artists who submitted designs. McNeel Marble Company of Marietta, Georgia, received the contract for the work. An account in *Confederate Veteran* describes it well: "There is no suggestion of the tumult of war in the structure. It is feminine and speaks silently but eloquently of the grief and self-sacrifice of the women of that period in giving up their husbands, sons, and brothers for the cause of the South." The monument was dedicated on May 1, 1913, in front of fifty women who had survived the war, as well as many Union and Confederate veterans. Robert L. Rogers was the orator of the day, and he "delivered an eloquent tribute to the women of the South during our tragic days of war and Reconstruction." Charles Coffin presented the monument to the state. The National Register of Historic Places added the monument to its list on April 26, 1996. The Arkansas Division of the Sons of Confederate Veterans and the United Daughters of the Confederacy celebrated the 100th anniversary of the monument as part of their 2013 Confederate Heritage Day on March 30.[87]

Platform

Monument Unveiling

Little Rock May 1, 1913

in Honor of

Confederate Women of Arkansas

1861-1865

Ribbon for the platform guest at the unveiling of the Little Rock Confederate Women's Monument on May 1, 1913. *Courtesy Old State House Museum Collection.*

Confederate Women of Arkansas statue on southeast corner of the state capitol grounds, circa 1913. *Courtesy of the Museum of the Confederacy, Richmond, Virginia.*

At the opposite end of the state capitol grounds is the Confederate soldiers monument, sculpted by Frederick Wellington Ruckstuhl (later Ruckstull). The cost of the monument was $10,000, and half of that was appropriated by the state while the rest was raised by UCV, UDC and SCV campaigns. One of the ways the Daughters raised its share was with its annual ball in December. The first one was held on December 15, 1898. The tickets were $2 per couple, but this event did not go far toward making the monument a reality. Finally, with the help of the legislature, the money was raised, and the monument was created.

Heavy storms delayed the unveiling, originally scheduled for May 5, 1905, and the dedication was rescheduled for Jefferson Davis's birthday, June 3. The celebration was lavish. It included a parade from Second and Center Streets to where the monument was located at the main entrance of the capitol building, which was still under construction. At the monument site, a band played "Dixie" as the red-and-white veiling was pulled away. Oratory filled the rest of the program, featuring speeches by State Representative Roy D. Campbell, who sponsored the appropriation bill for the monument; Governor Jeff Davis; Senator James H. Berry; and the orator of the day, Colonel Asa S. Morgan, who asserted that "the Confederate cause…is not lost, nor will the Confederate soldier be forgotten." In his closing remarks, Morgan summed up the message of monuments across the state and the South:

> *It devolves on you, Sons and Daughters of the Confederacy, and those who are to come after you, to cherish his memory, to preserve and keep alive the record of his glorious deeds. Let this sacred obligation sink deep into your hearts. At the foot of this monument tell the story of the Confederacy into the listening ears of your children until it becomes part of their nature to love, cherish, and defend the principles your fathers fought for, bled for, died for. Do not you slight them, for they are sacred now. Guard, shield, protect, and defend them from detraction, misrepresentation, and abuse, no matter whence it comes, and your children and your children's children in successive generations, looking back from the far-distant future, will proudly exclaim: "I am descended from a Confederate soldier!"*

Few, if any, orators anywhere in the South proclaimed the value and the purpose of the monument movement more succinctly than Colonel Morgan in this passage. The monument is listed on the National Register of Historic Places.[88]

Three other monuments in the Little Rock area deserve to be mentioned. The first two are on the grounds of the Old State House Museum, and they are similar in purpose, appearance and date of dedication. One is in memory of General William Read Scurry, and the other in memory of General Thomas J. Churchill. They were dedicated during the Thirty-ninth Annual Reunion of the Confederate Veterans held in Little Rock May 8–11, 1928. The Robert C. Newton Camp of the SCV placed both boulder monuments.

Scurry was from Gallatin, Tennessee, enlisted in the Texas Mounted Volunteers as a private in the Mexican War and was promoted to major. He served in the Texas Secession Convention and was an important officer in Texas Confederate forces. He was killed on April 30, 1864, at the Battle of Jenkins Ferry, Arkansas. He was buried in the state cemetery in Austin, Texas, in May 1864, and later, Texas dedicated a thirteen-foot-high white marble shaft over his grave.

Churchill was born near Louisville, Kentucky, in 1824 and served in the Mexican War with the First Kentucky Mounted Riflemen. After the war, he moved to Little Rock, where he married Ann Sevier, whom he had met while the Kentucky troops were stopped in Little Rock on the way to Mexico. When the Civil War began, he raised the First Arkansas Mounted Rifles and led it in the Battle of Wilson's Creek, Missouri. He was promoted to brigadier general in March 1862. He fought in several major battles in Arkansas and, after the war, returned to Little Rock and became involved in state politics. He served three terms as state treasurer and was elected governor in 1880. He was the major general of the Arkansas Division of the UCV in 1904. He died on May 14, 1905, and was buried with full military honors in Mount Holly Cemetery in Little Rock.[89]

These monuments stand today as permanent but subtle reminders of the most important event in our history. They have served to remind Americans of defeat, destruction and humiliation on the one hand, but they also help us recall the heritage and history of our region, our state, our community and the families whose men fought in the war for the beliefs they held as truth and whose women "kept the home fires burning." They still have stories to tell and lessons to teach. "Let us not forget" still has meaning today, as it is part of our history and cannot be erased or changed.

4

STILL TELLING WAR STORIES

GATHERING AROUND THE CAMPFIRES

As the Confederate veterans returned home after Appomattox, they nursed their wounds, reunited with their families, began to rebuild the devastated southern economy and infrastructure and worked to determine how to cope with the vast changes they saw all around them. There were no veterans' hospitals, no medical teams to treat illnesses or injuries, no knowledge of "post-traumatic stress disorder" or "Wounded Warriors" organizations to buffer the aftereffects of brutal war. They were on their own, as the federal government supplied no help to the former Confederates.

As a means of helping deal with the South that was vastly different from what they knew as they marched off to war, the veterans sought some degree of peace and solace by meeting with their old comrades in informal gatherings. As soldiers have done since warfare began, they reestablished the bonds they had forged on the battlefields and around campfires, in trenches and on marches, in hospitals and around fresh graves of friends and relatives.

At first, these gatherings were small and informal, but as the years passed, many of the local military units began to organize, elect officers and hold regularly scheduled annual meetings. A regional and eventually national organization, the United Confederate Veterans was established in 1889, and in 1896, the Sons of Confederate Veterans joined it in its commemorations of the veterans' service to the Confederacy. By the end of the century, these reunions were the primary source of Confederate memory and helped significantly to create and perpetuate the Lost Cause narrative and heritage.

The reunions, or encampments, as they were sometimes called, were similar in many respects. There were business meetings, with full slates of officers and committees. After the annual business was conducted, there were dinners, parades, campfires around which to tell war stories and bond with comrades and, of course, many speeches by local and unit orators. These orations, too, were often similar, praising the Confederate soldiers and sailors for their commitment, honor and heroics, defending the right of secession and states' rights and praising the women of the Confederacy who stayed at home and did all they could to support the war effort and keep their families alive and their farms or businesses functioning. Gradually, the orators began to acknowledge as well the need for national reconciliation and began to promote that reunion of the sections.

Reunions were still major events as late as 1911, forty-six years after Appomattox, even though the ranks were thinning as the old veterans passed away. Little Rock was the site of the 1911 reunion on May 16, 17 and 18, as the city of 45,000 expected about 50,000 visitors; more than 100,000 came to the capital city that week. All of the major railroads that served Little Rock added additional trains to accommodate the travelers. Major W.W. Screws, veteran and editor of the Montgomery, Alabama *Advertiser*, wrote, "Naturally there was doubt and misgiving as to whether or not it could handle such a crowd as usually attend these Reunions." But it worked out well, as the editor described it: "Doubt and misgiving gave way to satisfaction and pleasure when it was seen to what extent the people of Little Rock had opened their hearts and purses to give a few days' pleasure to the veterans of the gray."

Opening their hearts and purses required the establishment of forty-eight committees to take care of details, under the leadership of Judge W.M. Kavanaugh, who was the chair of the Executive Committee. Other key officers were H.C. Rather, treasurer, and George B. Brown, secretary.

One of the committees was the reunion lodging committee that scrambled to provide accommodations for the huge influx of veterans and families. They were placed in hotels, private homes, public school buildings and, finally, ten thousand of them in tents. The U.S. Army provided 1,300 tents and teams of soldiers to set them up in City Park, now MacArthur Park, near the arsenal. The tent city was called Camp Shaver and was named for Confederate officer Robert G. Shaver, who had commanded the Seventh Arkansas Infantry; he was also in charge of the tent camp. There were four giant dining tents set up with twenty-five cooks and sixty waiters who prepared and served fifty-four thousand meals that week. Twenty

Camp Shaver during the 1911 United Confederate Veterans reunion in Little Rock. *Courtesy of the UALR Center for Arkansas History and Culture.*

dishwashers were required to keep up with the flow of diners. A comment heard during the week was to the effect that if Lee had this much food for his troops, the war would have turned out differently.

It was decided early in the planning to house and feed the veterans at no charge to them. This commitment proved difficult. Businesses and citizens of the city were asked to pledge to a reunion fund, but in spite of the expected bonanza of spending by the friends and relatives of the veterans who would attend, pledges did not meet the needs. Finally, a Mr. Harry Ramey developed a plan to sell "dollar tribute buttons" across Arkansas. As the *Arkansas Democrat* described it: "It is the plan to sell the buttons all over the state, giving every man, woman and child in Arkansas an opportunity to contribute to the entertainment of the Confederate veterans." Ramey had a team of 250 women to campaign over the city to sell the buttons. He also wrote every school superintendent and officials in every county to ask for support in selling the buttons. Apparently it worked, as the newspaper reports and other accounts of the reunion indicate that the old veterans were well taken care of.

A highlight of the reunion was the reading of the letter to the veterans from President William H. Taft at the first business meeting. Taft wrote:

To the Confederate veterans who are now assembled in Little Rock, I send heartiest greetings and express the hope that they will have a pleasant and successful Reunion.

The men of the Confederate army fought for a principle which they believed to be right and for which they were willing to sacrifice their lives, their homes—in fact, all those things which men hold most dear. As we recognize their heroic services, so they and their descendants must honor the services rendered by the gallant sons of the North in the struggle for the preservation of the Union. The contending forces of nearly half a century ago have given place to a united North and South and to an enduring Union, in whose responsibilities and glorious destiny we equally and gratefully share.

During my visits South it has gratified me greatly to see those who fought for the blue and those who fought for the gray mingle together, worship the old flag, and feel a common pride in the deeds of heroism that were displayed in the Civil War. One of the most pleasant incidents of my visits through the South was the evident desire on the part of its people to confirm to the world that we are getting closer and closer together.

I congratulate the South on the wonderful progress which it is now making and on the spirit of civic pride which it is displaying.

The UCV made a quick reply to Taft:

The United Confederate Veterans' Association assembled at Little Rock, Ark., in annual convention, representing the Confederate survivors of the War Between the States, desire to express their appreciation of the kind telegram sent by you.

Viewed from either a personal or an official standpoint, it brings to the association greatest pleasure. It speaks volumes for the breadth and generosity of the sentiments the American people now hold of the gigantic conflict of 1861 to 1865 and the universal recognition that the men of the South fought for what they esteemed a great principle and which they backed by unfaltering courage.

This feeling plays a most important part in the restoration of perfect harmony and the confidence felt both by the North and the South. As brave men we are not unmindful of either the courage or patriotism of the Federal army. As of our own soldiers, we emphasize the achievements of those who followed the stars and stripes.

No patriot would change this spirit of peace and unbounded faith felt by all Americans in the superb destiny of the republic and which fills the hearts of all true men in every part of our country.

Intensely loyal to the memory of our gallant and chivalrous Confederate dead, we cheerfully accord those with whom we battled due praise for what they did in the course of the most dreadful war of modern times.

The UCV concludes with a statement of appreciation for Taft's decision while he was secretary of war to designate a plot in Arlington National Cemetery for the burial of Confederates "who died in prison or fell in the vicinity of Washington," and they thank him as well for his "appointment of many of our distinguished sons to high office."

The veterans and other visitors had many entertaining events scheduled for the nights after the business meetings were over. There were dances, receptions, plays and carnival-type attractions—such as snake shows, double-trapeze performers and a hot air balloon (although this one didn't get off the ground due to technical problems).

A key feature of the reunion was the dedication of the Capital Guards Monument in what is now MacArthur Park. When the Sixth Arkansas Infantry was formed, seventy-three men joined from Little Rock; only six returned from the war. Three of them were present at the unveiling. The monument was covered with twenty thousand roses, presumably in honor of the "City of Roses" nickname.

Over one hundred city streets were decorated with red, white and blue banners. Along the parade route and the distance from City Park to downtown, plaster columns were placed and lights were strung. Pictures of Confederate leaders like Lee and Davis where hung along the main thoroughfares.

The grand parade on the last day drew 150,000 spectators along the course, and they watched 12,000 veterans and fourteen bands pass by. The parade took almost two hours to pass a given point. Several hospital tents were set up along the route, and ambulances followed each division of the parade. The heat of mid-May in Little Rock caused some problems for the old veterans, but most made the full trip through the city.

The Veterans' Ball was the last event on the last night of the reunion. There were 5,800 who attended the four-hour dance party. The feature attraction at the ball was a precision drill exhibition by the Memphis Southern Cross Drill Corps. The dance ended with the singing of "Home, Sweet Home."

The *Arkansas Gazette* bragged that the city had "set herself the task of entertaining the old soldiers better than they have ever been entertained before." Apparently, the city felt it was a success, as the *Arkansas Democrat* editorialized that "the reunion is worth all its cost. It demonstrates that the

United Confederate Veterans reunion procession on Main Street in Little Rock in 1911. *Courtesy of the UALR Center for Arkansas History and Culture.*

spirit of Southern Chivalry still lives, that King Arthur and his Knights of the Table Round were no whit more brave and tender than are these old heroes of a conflict the likes of which has never before and will never again be seen."

As Ray Hanley points out in his thorough and compelling studies of the reunion, Little Rock used the event to attract attention and new businesses and residents. City leaders understood the impact the visitors could have, not just at the immediate time of the celebration, but also, if they were impressed enough, later as returning tourists and business owners who would move into the city. Little Rock was showcased and highlighted as a destination city in advertisements, brochures and other publications prior to and during the festivities. The three railroads—Frisco Lines; Nashville, Chattanooga & St. Louis Railway; and the Rock Island and Iron Mountain Railroad—all heavily promoted the reunion and offered special rates for their riders as they competed for the vastly increased business of that week.

In his welcoming speech, Little Rock mayor Charles E. Taylor pointed out to the city's visitors:

United Confederate Veterans reunion float with "Queen of the Reunion" and her maids in the procession down Main Street in Little Rock in 1911. *Courtesy of the UALR Center for Arkansas History and Culture.*

Little Rock is an up-to-date, stirring, progressive city, vying with other cities of the South and of the country in a wholesome rivalry as to accomplishment in those things which make cities great. In the development of our natural resources we are working out the same problems that confront a hundred other cities of the South. But we are learning the lesson in Little Rock that there are other resources than material that are of great value to us. We realize that, while we are building a city of factories, we must also build a city of homes; that while we are locating a new railroad, we should be building a new college and encourage the building of another church; that while we are offering inducements to the capitalist to invest his money with us, we must also offer to the poor young man from the country a city wherein he can rear his little family in comfort and peace and happiness; and, gentlemen, we are stopping to consider in Little Rock to-day whether we have not given just a little too much time to planning for a brilliant future for our city and too little time to studying the glorious past of our State and of our people. Your coming among us with the old veterans will set a new standard for our people in this matter, and Little Rock will be tremendously the gainer through your visit.

The veterans recognized and applauded their treatment and the success of the host city. Major W.W. Screws wrote in his Montgomery newspaper:

Little Rock is a modern commercial and manufacturing city. Veterans enter through the large and commodious passenger station from which streetcars and taxicabs carry them in all directions over smoothly paved streets, lined with substantial buildings. Several of the hotels are palatial, and many small ones are very comfortable. The public buildings are elaborate and private homes among the most attractive in the South.

Colonel John P. Hickman, adjutant general of the Army of Tennessee, wrote in *Confederate Veteran*:

It has been my good fortune to attend every Reunion of the United Confederate Veterans...I have never visited any city more elaborately decorated in Confederate colors than was Little Rock...Independent of the decorations, we had the hearts of all of the people. They were glad to receive us, and want us again.

Many favorable comments also came from Arkansas veterans. John W. Bratcher, commander of the Sterling Price Camp of the UCV in Waldron, wrote to the *Confederate Veteran*: "I have just returned from the Reunion of the veterans at Little Rock. That city cannot receive too much praise for the manner in which it managed the entire reunion…This Reunion is said to be the best of all. Hurrah for Arkansas!"

Another interesting aspect of the reunion was the presence of black southerners who had participated in the war in one way or another—doing menial work around camps, cooking, driving teams of horses or mules, digging and preparing defenses and aiding their owners as they fought and were in camp. These men attended the UCV reunions from the beginning of the organization. As the reunion broke up, these black veterans met and passed a resolution thanking the people of Little Rock for their hospitality:

> *We are gathered here today to give thanks to the good people of the city for their kind treatment toward the Negro veterans. We have met with many reunions but we would like to say the Lord lives in Little Rock…If I were permitted to do so I would change the name of Little Rock to "Little Rock Paradise" or the "Paradisiacal City."*

There was a touch of sadness to the final closing of the reunion as the old veterans realized that many would not be at the 1912 reunion. Four had died while in Little Rock, and their ranks were thinning rapidly. One writer in the *Southern Standard*, the Arkadelphia newspaper, summed up the event: "We, accompanied by our wife attended the Confederate Reunion in Little Rock, and we have attended many reunions, but we must say, that this one, was one of the best and best conducted and arranged one we ever before attended." He went on to remark that he had "heard many an old Vet praising Little Rock for the royal manner in which they were entertained." The writer concluded his piece with the sad observation: "In a few more years, there will be none left to attend a reunion."[90]

The truth in this statement was obvious when the UCV next met in Little Rock May 8–11, 1928, when only 1,098 delegates registered for their credentials. The state had appropriated $3,000, and Little Rock added an additional $1,500; this level of support ensured that the UCV selected Little Rock at its 1927 convention in Tampa. This contribution was recognized as the first time a state legislature had appropriated any amount to support a UCV reunion. Atlanta had been in the running, but when the Atlanta delegation heard of the state's appropriation, John Ashley Jones of Atlanta withdrew in favor of the City of Roses. He told the convention, however, that Atlanta would bid for the reunion the next year and "intends to have it

Arkansas Asks You To Come

Come to our great Reunion.
  Meet with the "Boys in Gray,"
  They fought a brave fight
  Thru the South's darkest night.
  Then let's honor them while we may.

Come to the next Reunion;
  See Arkansas in her pride;
  A welcome you'll find,
  Of that heart-to-heart kind,
  That will glad you on every side.

Come to our grand Reunion.
  Your Youth and your Veterans all bring;
  For happy we'll be,
  Every old friend to see;
  Hail Dixie! Ho Dixie! Come join us and sing.

—*Josie Frazee Cappleman.*

Thirty-eighth Reunion
United Confederate Veterans
GEN. J. C. FOSTER, *Commander-in-Chief*
Houston, Texas

Thirty-third Convention
Sons of Confederate Veterans
DR. SUMTER L. LOWRY, *Commander-in-Chief*
Tampa, Florida

Twenty-ninth Convention
Confederated Southern Memorial Association
MRS. A. McD. WILSON, *President General*
Atlanta, Georgia

Little Rock, Arkansas — May 8 to 11, 1928

CENTRAL PRINTING CO., LITTLE ROCK

Brochure for 1928 UCV reunion in Little Rock. *Courtesy Old State House Museum Collection.*

that year if we have to whip everybody to get it." The speculation was that the Stone Mountain Memorial would be near completion at that time and would be a significant part of the reunion program.

Little Rock immediately set to work establishing thirty-one committees with Colonel E.R. Wiles, the general chairman of the Reunion Committee. The UCV believed his "large experience in the affairs of the SCV eminently fits him for leadership in carrying out the big plans which the occasion demands of high ideals of the chivalry of the Old South." Wiles was viewed as "approachable and dependable," and it was anticipated that "every phase of the great gathering will be taken care of."

After some speculation that the historic Mississippi River flood of 1927 would lead to the cancellation of the 1928 reunion, Wiles wrote an open letter to *Confederate Veteran* magazine:

> *We are looking forward with joyous anticipation to the arrival of the gray hosts and allied organization next year. There is nothing that will be left undone to make their stay in our midst one to be remembered as long as they live. The Fair Park adjoining the city, one of the most beautiful locations to be found west of the Mississippi River, will be headquarters for the reunion. All veterans who desire it will be fed and housed in warm, dry buildings, with the best of facilities of every kind, and will be fed in mess halls adjacent, free of cost to them…Side trips to Hot Springs, the oil fields, and other points of interest will be arranged over the railroad leading out of here. The general headquarters of the Confederate veterans will be at the Hotel Marion, and Sons of Confederate Veterans at Hotel LaFayette. Reservations should be sent in at once.*

Some of the plans regarding the "warm, dry buildings" must have been shelved or were overwhelmed by the numbers of unexpected veterans who came into town or reserved a spot, as a May article in *Confederate Veteran* pointed out that three hundred army tents would be set up to "supplement the housing facilities at the Fair Park."

Little Rock remembered the public relations strategies of the 1911 reunion, and an essay in *Confederate Veteran* reminded the veterans of some of the advantages of the city:

> *Little Rock is the metropolis of the "Wonder State," and a worthy center of interest, with its natural advantages added to those which have come through commercial and industrial expansion…*

Schedule and Rates to

LITTLE ROCK, ARKANSAS

38th Annual Reunion United Confederate Veterans

May 8th to 11th, 1928

Leave Kansas City or St. Louis May 7th

FROM KANSAS CITY		FROM ST. LOUIS	
Leave Kansas City, Mo. Pac.	4:30 P.M.	Leave St. Louis, Mo. Pac.	10:30 P.M.
Arrive Little Rock	7:30 A.M.	Arrive Little Rock	7:40 A.M.
Round trip fare	$17.18	Round trip fare	$12.59
Lower Berth, one way	5.63	Lower Berth, one way	4.13
Upper Berth, one way	4.50	Upper Berth, one way	3.30
Drawing Room, one way	21.00	Drawing Room, one way	15.00

THE MISSOURI PACIFIC RAILROAD IS THE OFFICIAL ROUTE AND WILL OPERATE SPECIAL MISSOURI DIVISION SLEEPING CARS.

Railroad broadside advertising ticket prices for 1928 UCV reunion in Little Rock. *Courtesy Old State House Museum Collection.*

It is a city of beautiful homes and handsome public buildings. Five bridges span the Arkansas River, connecting the two parts of the city. Two of these bridges, costing more than three million dollars, are memorials to the men of the army and navy who died in the World War. The beautiful Fair Park, with its buildings of Colonial architecture, draws more than two hundred thousand vacationists for the "Second Week in October." This park is a beautiful grove of native trees, two hundred and thirty acres in extent, and makes the world's "Most beautiful fair grounds." Over a million dollars was expended in converting the original wilderness into a beauty spot that will be a joy forever to the people of the city…

Of schools, the city has an extensive public school system, with an enrollment of more than 17,000 annually, and in addition there is the Little Rock College, the Medical Department of the University of Arkansas, and the Law School…

Altogether, it is a city which offers many advantages, and, to be appreciated most, has to be seen, and what better time to visit there than during the Confederate reunion? Comrades, don't fail to be there.

The article ends with a boost for Hot Springs: "Hot Springs National Park is within a few hours' ride of Little Rock, and will welcome visitors during the reunion." The article mentions De Soto's expedition in the area, points out the building of the first bathhouse in 1830 and the 1877 act of Congress that created the second National Park in the United States. It praises the "resort of thousands of visitors annually who find the baths beneficial." Doubtless, some of the old veterans experienced the baths before returning home.

But before they left Little Rock, they wrapped up the reunion with the annual grand parade, which started in North Little Rock on Park Hill and concluded in downtown Little Rock on Main Street. Some veterans walked the parade route, others were on horseback, while most rode in cars: "They like open cars, some riding Lindbergh fashion, so they might see the crowds and drink in their adulation." There were one thousand cars and other vehicles in the parade, more than six thousand people and eighteen bands from around the South. According to the press reports, it was over five miles long and took over an hour to pass a given point.

The 1928 reunion was another success for Little Rock and the "Wonder State." It had thoroughly entertained over one thousand survivors of the Civil War and thousands more of their families and friends. The youngest veteran for whom there was a record was seventy-eight years old, and the oldest was ninety-nine.[91]

Little Rock hosted one more UCV reunion on September 27–29, 1949. Only four veterans were able to attend. The UCV believed at the time that only twenty-eight Confederates were still alive in 1949. The Marion Hotel was again the headquarters for the reunion. Governor Sid McMath proclaimed "Confederate Week" and directed that the Confederate flag be flown in public places around the city.

One of the veterans, General James W. Moore, the ninety-eight-year-old commander of the UCV, claimed that he was the only person still living who had attended Robert E. Lee's 1870 funeral. Thomas E. Riddle, who came to the reunion from Wichita Falls, Texas, complained that there was no entertainment, and he was going to go back home. But there was some entertainment, as the U.S. Marine Band presented several concerts, and the UDC had a breakfast for the final Confederate soldiers.

Postcard of U.S. Marine Band in the parade at the 1928 UCV reunion in Little Rock. *Courtesy Old State House Museum Collection.*

There were two more UCV reunions in 1950 and 1951. That ended the long run of memory and commemoration of the war years for the veterans, but their tradition and heritage is still ably carried on by other heritage organizations. The Sons of Confederate Veterans (founded in 1896), the United Daughters of the Confederacy (established in 1894) and the Military Order of the Stars and Bars (created in 1938) are still honorably and tirelessly promoting the story of the Confederacy, the Lost Cause and the heritage and history of the South, as we will see in the next chapter.

There were, of course, many other Confederate veterans' reunions around the state of Arkansas. Most of these were small, local, unit-sized encampments, but the general purposes were the same as the larger, regional and national reunions of the UCV. The organizers of these UCV and SCV camps aimed to preserve and enhance the friendships created in the hard times of war; to provide for less fortunate soldiers who might have lost an arm or a leg or who were having difficult financial times; and to preserve and pass on the southern soldiers' perspective on the history and heritage of the Old South, the Confederacy, the war and the postwar years. A brief survey will highlight some of these events around Arkansas.

The Clarksville John F. Hill UCV Camp was especially diligent in sponsoring reunions, and the Johnson County Historical Society is equally adept at collecting and preserving the records and photographs of these events. The local newspaper, the *Herald-Democrat*, published unusually thorough and detailed accounts of the day's activities over the years.

Photo from the 1949 UCV reunion on the Old State House lawn. *Courtesy Old State House Museum Collection.*

May 10, 1920, was "clear and beautiful," and the ladies of the Felix I. Batson chapter of the UDC "were busy all the fore-noon arranging a bountiful spread for the Veterans." The meal was held at the Methodist Church, and after an "hour of social concourse and a splendid dinner," the Veterans were "motored to the speakers stand, near the soldiers burial ground." Congressman T.H. Caraway was the orator of the day; his "address was of unusual interest, interspersed by many witticisms. He dwelt much on the importance of every soldier supplying historians as early as possible, with facts concerning the war, that it may be recorded before there are none left to tell." After Caraway's conclusion, seventeen boys dressed in scout uniforms and seventeen girls in white placed flags and flowers on the Confederate lot. The ceremony was concluded with the Citizens Band playing "Dixie," which, the newspaper pointed out, "never fails to bring forth a yell of appreciation from the old soldiers." Most of the soldiers buried in Oakland Cemetery had died in 1862 in local hospitals and had served in Thomas Churchill's Regiment.[92]

Searcy, in White County, had an ideal gathering place for reunions. Spring Park had "hotels nearby, cool shade, good water, and plenty of room." Since the encampments were held in August, the "cool shade" had to be appealing. The first two annual meetings of the veterans in the area were at Gum Springs in 1895, when the L.M. Walker Camp 687 formed with seventy-five members, and at Center Hill, ten miles west of Searcy. Searcy then became the designated spot, and the veterans enjoyed the "cool shade and good water" until the last reunion in 1929, when only four veterans were able to attend.[93]

The Jackson County association of Confederate Veterans met for the first time on June 29, 1889, in Newport and "had a rousing old time here," according to the newspaper story. M.M. Stuckey "delivered an eloquent and soul stirring address," and the group unanimously passed a resolution inviting all Union soldiers to meet with the camp in future gatherings. The first reunion of the groups was held in 1893 at a grove called "the Island" on a plantation owned by Samuel Anthony. The next year, the camp held the reunion there but, in 1895, moved it to old Elizabeth, which had been the county seat from 1839 to 1852. Not much of the town site was left, as it was in a flood-prone area, but the encampments were held in a meadow between the White River and the Black River and became known as the "Confederate Campgrounds." The reunions were three days long, and an account describes the 1893 event:

Many of the Federal soldiers living in the county have been invited to participate in the three days of camp life and talk over war days and deeds of valor. It is hoped that the old gray-haired vets who wore the gray, and their guests who wore the blue, some of whom are vets of two wars, will have a most pleasant time during this, their first encampment.[94]

The first Confederate reunion in Washington County was held in September 1886 at Prairie Grove, the site of one of the largest battles of the war in Arkansas. Planning had started on March 19 with a letter signed by twenty-one veterans that called for a meeting "to consider the propriety of having an ex-Confederate reunion." A meeting was held at Prairie Grove on July 3 to discuss holding the reunion in September; fifty-nine veterans attended, and they elected officers. W.B. Blanton was elected president, and an executive committee was established. An invitation was extended to all ex-Federals and to all others who had fought at Prairie Grove. The reunion was held, and an account of the program called it a "great event." It has continued in various forms for over a century.[95]

The Ben T. Embry Camp No. 977 met in its annual meeting at Gravel Hill in Pope County on August 1, 1906. Out of a membership of 292, 78 members were present, and the minutes reflected that "caused us to realize that we too, are nearing the last roll-call, and soon it will be said of us, that:

On Fame's eternal camping ground
Their silent tents are spread,
And glory guards with solemn sound
The bivouac of the dead.

The camp was then entertained by Captain W.W. Bailey, "in his usual attractive manner, reviewing the history of the past, the dissolution of a republic, with contending armies demanding what they deemed to be just and right; and then a restoration to peace, a contented, happy and prosperous people." After his oration, dinner was served. The afternoon session was filled with the recitation of an original composition by Miss Donie Tussler of Lutherville entitled "The Confederate Veteran"; the orator of the day, J.T. Bullock, who gave "one of his splendid efforts"; and several shorter speeches by various members of the camp. A memorial resolution was passed and read, remembering the twelve members of the camp who had died in the past year.[96]

Forrest City hosted several reunions in the early 1900s at Stuart Springs, a local park. The barbecue in September 1902 listed seventy-three veterans

Civil War Confederate Soldiers reunion in Prairie Grove in 1886. *Courtesy Shiloh Museum of Ozark History/Dr. Calvin Bain Collection (S-2006-21-36).*

Confederate Veterans reunion in Prairie Grove in 1897. *Courtesy Shiloh Museum of Ozark History/Mildred Carnahan Collection (S-98-2-569).*

ranging in age from fifty-seven to eighty. The 1907 reunion listed only forty-five veterans; death was taking its toll.[97]

As Congressman Caraway discussed at his oration in Clarksville, mentioned above, one of the major goals of the UCV was to collect, preserve and disseminate a history of Arkansas during the war. At the Lonoke reunion in 1906, considerable time was spent by S.H. Nowlin from Little Rock, who was the chairman of the historical committee for the Arkansas Division of the UCV, talking to the veterans and others about materials to which they might have access. Apparently, he must have been successful, as he stayed two extra days to talk with people in Lonoke. He received from Congressman Joe T. Robinson of Lonoke the original muster roll of Company H, Twenty-fourth Arkansas Infantry, dating from October 1 to December 31, 1862. An appeal went out from the *Lonoke Weekly Democrat* for "anyone who can assist in these matters of gathering information" to please contact Major Nowlin or the newspaper office.[98]

A final example is the Bentonville reunion in 1893. In a letter to the *Confederate Veteran* magazine, J. Montgomery Wilson of Springfield, Missouri, writes of his experiences at the reunion: "I am not capable of describing the pleasure manifested by the old veterans in meeting once more, many of them for the first time in twenty-eight years. It was a continuous love feast, and when it closed they lingered around, seeming in no hurry to leave. It was good to be there." He then reports on the speeches he heard and tells us about one of the key elements in these events that made them so important to southern history: the respect and honor Confederate veterans paid to the women of the South, who were so important to the war effort and to the recovery period after Appomattox: "Nearly every one of the speakers touched upon the heroism of our Southern women during the war. There was scarcely a dry eye in the audience…God bless the women of the South who lived during the four years' strife. The Spartan women we read of in history never went through one-half what they did… Girls of the present day should know of the heroic deeds of their mothers and grandmothers. I think it would kindle within them flames of loftiest patriotism."[99]

As this brief survey has shown, Arkansas's veterans' reunions went a long way promoting the Confederate heritage and history of the state. The often-repeated messages and ceremonies explaining why the South lost the war, praising the heroism and sacrifice of the soldiers and sailors and honoring the strength and courage of the women all evoked and reinforced the creation of Civil War memory in the state. Today, in the twenty-first century, the SCV, UDC, MOS&B and other southern heritage groups are carrying on this tradition and doing what they can to strengthen this public memory and protect this heritage for future generations.

KEEPING THE HERITAGE ALIVE

ARKANSAS'S CIVIL WAR HERITAGE IN THE TWENTY-FIRST CENTURY

As we have seen, Arkansas did its share in building and sustaining the memory of the Civil War through Confederate Memorial Day commemorations, dedications of Confederate memorials and monuments and the reunions of Confederate veterans' organizations, just as the other states of the Confederacy did. The public memory that was created through the oratory and the ritual of these often-repeated events built a strong foundation and heritage that is still with us today. As the 150th anniversary progresses, the interest in the hundreds of sites in Arkansas related to the Civil War will doubtless increase, and there are several important agencies and groups promoting and supporting that interest. I will take a look at several currents flowing through the state in the early part of the twenty-first century that are keeping alive our important Civil War heritage.

Perhaps the most important step occurred in 2007, when the Arkansas General Assembly created the Arkansas Civil War Sesquicentennial Commission (ACWSC). This commission is a program of the Arkansas Historic Preservation Program, an agency of the Department of Arkansas Heritage. The duties of this program include the planning and carrying out of appropriate programs and activities that will "ensure the commemoration results in a positive legacy and has long-term public benefits." The commission promotes and facilitates interdisciplinary study of the Civil War, encourages organizations around the state to participate in "activities to expand the understanding and appreciation of the significance of the Civil War," facilitates the "distribution of scholarly research, publications, and interpretations of the Civil War" and provides "technical assistance to local organizations and nonprofit organizations to

The SCV and UDC members after the ceremony at the Arkansas state capitol rotunda on Confederate Memorial Day, March 30, 2013. *Courtesy of W. Stuart Towns.*

further the commemoration of the sesquicentennial." The commission's mission is to "support a statewide observance of the 150th anniversary of the American Civil War that is educational, comprehensive and inclusive; that tells the story of the Civil War in Arkansas without making judgments about the actions and motivations of the people who took part in the war, and that stresses the relevance to Arkansawyers today by promoting local observances and acknowledging the impact the Civil War had on modern Arkansas."[100] As we reach the halfway point of the sesquicentennial, it is easy to see the success the ACWSC has had across the state.

An example of the support and publicity provided by this commission is the monthly schedule published in local newspapers around the state that lists and describes various Civil War events, such as the "Fought in Earnest" Civil War Arkansas traveling exhibit that the Arkansas History Commission created and that is circulating throughout the state to libraries, museums and other venues throughout the sesquicentennial commemoration. The current list through the end of the sesquicentennial can be found on the ACWSC's website at www.arkansascivilwar150.com/events.

Arkansas can claim the fourth-highest number of offensive military operations during the Civil War. Only Virginia, Tennessee and Missouri had more military activity between 1861 and the end of the war four years later. Several battles were fought, including Pea Ridge, Prairie Grove, Jenkins Ferry, Chalk Bluff, Ditch Bayou, Prairie D'Anne, Arkansas Post, Marks Mill and Helena, as well as hundreds of skirmishes and other military actions around the state. During the sesquicentennial, many descendants of the soldiers who were involved in these actions will come to Arkansas to see where their ancestors served the Union or the Confederacy. The rapid growth and interest in historical and cultural tourism across the state is having an impact.

These visitors are like many Americans who are earning the name "Heritage Tourists," due to their interest in historical and cultural sites and activities. According to a survey by the Civil War Preservation Trust and reported by Mark Christ of the Arkansas Historic Preservation Program, these travelers are mostly in their late forties or early fifties, well educated, with household incomes between $61,200 and $79,500. They spend an average of $50 per person per day and thus bring money into local economies while requiring few municipal costs. City leaders around the state are recognizing this boon to local economies and are capitalizing on it.

A specific example of the benefits a Civil War battlefield site can bring to a community is shown by the Civil War Preservation Trust's study of the economic benefits of the Prairie Grove battlefield, now an Arkansas State Park. In 2005, battlefield visitors, of whom 56 percent were tourists, spent $2.1 million in the local area and generated $72,000 in local and $210,000 in state taxes. Forty-one percent of the visitors came to the area specifically to see the battlefield, and those who stayed overnight stayed an average of two nights. Seventy-five percent thought the Prairie Grove site superior to other battlefields they had visited, and 90 percent would recommend it to their friends. With those kinds of figures, it is easy to see how financially important the remembrance of the Civil War can be to a community in addition to the quality of historical information and understanding passed on to families and young people.

The Arkansas Civil War Sesquicentennial Commission developed an annual theme for each of the five years of the observance. According to Mark Christ, the themes cover the major issues the state faced during those war years a century and a half ago. The 2011 theme was "Why Commemorate the Civil War?" The goal was to encourage state citizens and visitors to reflect on the reasons for war and the impacts of war on a nation. The idea was to explore and pass on the relevance of the events of the Civil War 150 years ago to our citizens a century and a half later.

In 2012, the theme was "A Divided Arkansas," and the goal was to examine the invasion of the state by Federal forces and the Confederate government's authorized formations of guerrilla fighters across the state to oppose them. Some citizens tried to stay out of the conflict, but many other families were split as members pledged allegiance to one side or the other. As the war wore on, every community in the state was affected.

The 2013 theme is "Big War, Little War" and focuses on the anguish of the thousands of Arkansas soldiers sent to fight far from home east of the Mississippi River and the hardships faced by those who stayed back in Arkansas. In addition, in 1863, there were many choices and issues faced by the state's African Americans, who had to decide whether to stay with their owners or escape to the Union forces occupying the state.

In 2014, the state will focus on the theme "Under Two Governments," which examines the situation in which there was a Union and a Confederate government in the state that attempted to deal with the rapid depletion of food and other supplies and the lawlessness of a state wracked by guerrilla warfare. Bands of armed men roamed the state killing and stealing what they wanted, and the dual governments were not able to control them.

In the final year of the sesquicentennial, the theme is "Emancipation and Reconstruction," which will examine the year the Confederacy surrendered and former Confederate soldiers returned to the state. These veterans, often wounded or otherwise suffering from the trauma of war, were forced to live with the devastated environment that was so different socially and economically than what they had left four years before.

The Sesquicentennial Commission's website, www.arkansascivilwar150. com, includes information on sites across the state, preservation opportunities, cellphone tours and a database of every regiment that fought in the state, as well as the schedule of the traveling exhibit that will circulate around the state during the period. There are also research and education subpages that include, among other things, an Arkansas Civil War timeline, an Arkansas Civil War bibliography, a database that lists every battle fought in the state, children's activities related to the Civil War and other research information.

The ACWSC has also developed several other important programs, one of which is the historical marker program that is aimed at placing at least one sesquicentennial marker in each of the state's seventy-five counties by the end of the sesquicentennial period. The commission will fund up to $1,100 per marker, and the local area provides the remainder of the average cost of $2,030. The commission will verify the accuracy of each marker. County and city governments, historical societies, local museums, heritage organizations— such as the UDC and SCV—as well as individual citizens are underwriting the local share of these markers. (See the appendix for the current list of completed historical markers as of September 19, 2013.)

An example of this program is the dedication ceremony for a Civil War marker at Camp Ground United Methodist Church, just northwest of Paragould in Greene County. It was held on September 7, 2013. The Greene County Historical and Genealogical Society, the James Wiseman Honnoll Chapter of the UDC, Mitchell Adair Chapter of the Children of the Confederacy, the Robert Shaver Camp of the SCV, reenactors of the Thirtieth Arkansas Infantry, the Arkansas Division of the SCV and the Military Order of the Stars and Bars participated in the dedication. W. Danny Honnoll, commander of the Army of Trans-Mississippi of the Sons of Confederate Veterans and a member of the Arkansas Civil War Sesquicentennial Commission, conducted the ceremony, along with Captain M. Ray Jones III, Arkansas Division of the SCV commander. The commemoration included laying flowers in honor of Confederate dead by Bobbie Barnett of Ravenden, representing the Mother of Civil War Veterans and escorted by Lieutenant Harold Hunt. In his speech, Honnoll said:

Today, we take justifiable pride in our Confederate forebears, men and women, who sacrificed their all for the cause in which they believed. The Confederate soldier won the admiration of the world by his courageous fight against an enemy overwhelming in numbers, equipment and implements of war. With few exceptions they were volunteers who fought for principles of government in which they believed. Although defeated, they left us traditions of faith in God, honor, chivalry and respect for womanhood; they left us passionate belief in freedom for the individual. Our Confederate ancestors bequeathed to us a military tradition of valor, patriotism, devotion to duty and spirit of self-sacrifice. When our nation no longer admires and pays tribute to these traditions, we will no longer remain a free nation.

The marker reads:

5th Arkansas Infantry Regiment was organized on
June 28, 1861, at Gainesville about seven miles
northwest of modern day Paragould. Men from
Greene County served in Companies C, D, E, and H.
The Soldiers trained and camped near the springs at
Camp Ground United Methodist Church.
Transferred east of the Mississippi River, the 5th
Arkansas Regiment fought with the Army of
Tennessee in Mississippi, Kentucky, Tennessee,
Georgia and North Carolina, earning the nickname

"The Fighting Fifth." The casualty depleted 5th merged with ten other regiments in 1865.[101]

Another program aimed at the heritage tourists traveling in Arkansas is the Civil War Passport Program that has twenty-three passport stamping stations and thirty-eight associated sites around the state. The northwest Arkansas stamping stations are Pea Ridge National Military Park, Prairie Grove Battlefield State Park, Fort Smith National Historic Site and the Buffalo National River, Tyler Bend Visitor Center. In northeast Arkansas, Jacksonport State Park, Randolph County Heritage Museum and the Piggott Visitor Center are stamping stations. In central Arkansas, visitors can get their passports stamped at the Jacksonville Museum of Military History, the Old State House Museum, the MacArthur Museum of Arkansas Military History, the Plantation Agricultural Museum, the Grant County Museum and the Pine Bluff/Jefferson County Museum. Stamping stations in southeast Arkansas are at Arkansas Post National Memorial, St. Charles Museum, Delta Cultural Center, Phillips County Museum, Lakeport Plantation and Lake Chicot State Park. Southwest Arkansas's passport stations are at Historic Washington State Park, Nevada County Museum, McCollum-Chidester House and the White Oak Lake State Park. The thirty-eight associated sites can be found on the Arkansas Civil War Sesquicentennial Commission website.

A final outstanding program by the ACWSC is the Grant Program, which awards matching grants up to $2,000 for local programs, exhibits, reenactments and similar events for activities taking place from 2011 through 2015. There are various deadlines for grant proposals listed on the commission's website. Some of the recent grants include projects in Pulaski, Hempstead, Union and Benton Counties. They are for varied activities, such as the return of the flag of the Third Iowa Cavalry to the MacArthur Museum of Arkansas Military History; the seventh annual Red River Heritage Symposium, "The Home Front"; the 2nd Chance @ Life Emancipation Committee in El Dorado for the 2013 Juneteenth celebration; and the Heritage Trail Partners Inc. in Rogers to refurbish the Battle of Dunagin's Farm historical marker.[102]

Helena–West Helena has earned praise for its efforts to promote and commemorate the sesquicentennial and attract the heritage tourist. The city's heritage includes Union occupation, a battle to bring the city back under Confederate control, seven Confederate generals from the city and a camp of several thousand freed slaves who had come to Helena after the Federal occupation and were freed by the Union commander General Samuel Curtis. The city's approach is to take a broad interpretive view of

Civil War marker dedication at Camp Ground United Methodist Church on September 14, 2013. *Courtesy of W. Stuart Towns.*

the war in Helena–West Helena. A brochure on the city and the Civil War asserts, "This is the story of our nation's struggle. This is our history." It is obvious from its programs that Helena–West Helena means for those "our" references to include all Americans and all southerners, white and black.

The city's major project was the building and dedication of a large Union fort replica in May 2012. This project was the outgrowth of a strategic plan for Phillips County devised in 2005 that identified the Civil War as an important heritage resource. Over the next few years, the community supported the idea of making Helena–West Helena a Civil War tourism destination that would speak to the history of both black and white citizens who were affected by the war years. Fort Curtis was the first result, but by 2013, the city had identified several Civil War sites, such as Federal gun batteries on Crowley's Ridge above the city, the Confederate Cemetery plot overlooking the Mississippi River—which features many Confederate graves of soldiers killed during the Battle of Helena on July 4, 1863—as well as the monument to General Patrick Cleburne at his grave and the monument to Confederate soldiers. An impressive bronze statue of Cleburne was dedicated in front of the Phillips County Museum in 2013, and the SCV commemorates his birthday at his monument and grave in March each year.

Bronze statue of General Patrick Cleburne in front of Helena–West Helena Museum.
Courtesy of W. Stuart Towns.

Possibly the most important part of this strategic plan to make Helena–West Helena a heritage tourist destination is Freedom Park, dedicated in 2013. This park, a few blocks south of Fort Curtis, includes five major exhibits that describe the African American experience in the city during the Civil War, when they moved into the city by the thousands as fugitive slaves. They were labeled contraband for a time, but they were granted their freedom. Some of the men joined the USCT (United States Colored Troops) and served in the Union forces. Unfortunately, thousands of those who followed the Union into Helena died of disease and malnutrition, as their numbers overwhelmed the Union logistics capabilities. Freedom Park tells this story well and is a significant example of the ACWSC's goal to tell the story of everyone affected by the war across Arkansas.

Estavan Hall, the oldest house remaining in Helena, will become a visitor's center and illustrate how the war and the Union occupation of Helena affected the families and other citizens left behind when the men went to war.

Two of the leading Civil War organizations have recently been established in Helena–West Helena. The Seven Generals Camp of the Sons of Confederate Veterans was organized in early 2013 and meets on a regular basis. The Civil War Roundtable of the Delta also began operations in 2013 and holds monthly meetings.

The latest development in Helena–West Helena in this campaign for heritage tourism is the purchase by the Sons of Confederate Veterans of about an acre of land overlooking Fort Curtis and next to a Civil War–era home, the Moore-Hornor residence. It is located at the spot where the Confederate troops broke through the Federal lines before being pushed back during the Battle of Helena. It will be called the "Confederate Memorial Park" and is intended to complement and provide the Confederate balance to the Union Fort Curtis and the African American Freedom Park projects. Much like many of the earlier monument and cemetery projects of the United Confederate Veterans and United Daughters of the Confederacy, the Seven Generals Camp of the SCV conducted a fundraising campaign, but this one used the Internet to help fund the project, not barbecues, plays, concerts or lectures as in the past efforts.[103]

The Arkansas Department of Parks and Tourism has created a Civil War Heritage Trail that highlights various routes taken by Union or Confederate troops as they moved through the state. Many of the most important battles, skirmishes and other Civil War operations and sites are on these trails and are featured on the map shown here. The Department of Parks and Tourism has erected signs to provide continuity and to enable heritage tourists to easily follow their routes to see the various Civil War sites around the state.

Exhibit of the U.S. Colored Troops at Freedom Park in Helena–West Helena. *Courtesy of W. Stuart Towns.*

Civil War Heritage Trail sign. *Courtesy of W. Stuart Towns.*

CIVIL WAR TRAILS

Civil War trails. *Courtesy of Arkansas Department of Parks and Tourism.*

Like the arrangement of the Confederate monument locations around Arkansas in chapter three, the Civil War Trail is divided into the northwest, northeast, southeast, southwest and central areas of the state. The map can be found at tourist centers around the state and on the Department of Parks and Tourism website at www.arkansasheritagetrails.com.

An example of a half-day tour to visit Civil War sites in Arkansas would be eight locations in the Little Rock area, as described by Jack Schnedler in the *Arkansas Democrat-Gazette*. The tour is outlined in a brochure available at tourist destinations around the state or downloaded from www.civilwarbuff.org. It includes the MacArthur Museum of Arkansas Military History in MacArthur Park; Reed's Bridge at Bayou Meto, east of Jacksonville, where Confederate forces held out successfully against Federal units and where there is a group of five Civil War–era buildings at Reed's Bridge Family Farm Settlement; Brownsville Cemetery, off AR 131 north of Lonoke, where Confederates were overwhelmed by Federal troops on August 25, 1863; Ashley's Mills near Scott Plantation

Southern Confederate Heritage Park in Jonesboro. *Courtesy of W. Stuart Towns.*

Settlement, where heavy fighting occurred on September 7–9, 1863; a marker at Willow Beach Lake where Union forces built a wooden pontoon bridge; Pratt Cates Remmel Park, on Lindsey Road, the site of "the Battle Before the Fall of Little Rock"; a granite marker at the intersection of Fourche Dam Pike and East Roosevelt Road that notes where Union troops defeated Confederates in the Battle of Little Rock; Riverfront Park, where there are two markers depicting the victorious Union campaign to take Little Rock on September 11, 1863; and the final stop is near the intersection of U.S. 70 and AR 165 in North Little Rock, where Confederate generals John S. Marmaduke and Lucius M. Walker fought a duel in which General Walker was killed.[104]

Two other events in north-central Arkansas continue the long history of veterans' reunions in the state. In Heber Springs, the celebration is called the "Old Soldiers Reunion for Veterans of All Wars," and on August 1–3, 2013, the sponsors organized its 126th meeting. In the early years, it was called the "Reunion of the Blue and Gray." The American Legion Saxton-Willis Post No. 64, the Unit No. 64 Ladies Auxiliary and the Post No. 64 Sons of the American Legion maintain the event today in Spring Park. It is claimed to be the "oldest veterans gathering of its type west of the Mississippi," according to Chuck McCracken of Heber Springs, the parade chairman.[105]

In Mammoth Spring State Park, near the Missouri state line, the "Old Soldiers, Sailors, Marines, and Air Force Reunion" is conducted by the local VFW Post Forest-Stone No. 7831 and its Ladies Auxiliary. Not quite as long

Southern Confederate Heritage Park sign. *Courtesy of W. Stuart Towns.*

running as the event in Heber Springs, the city has been host to the veterans since 1893.[106]

A final example out of many contemporary events and commemorations in Arkansas is the Southern Confederate Heritage Park at 117 Southwest Drive in Jonesboro. It belongs to the North East Arkansas Southern Heritage Foundation, which is composed of members of the James Wiseman Honnoll Chapter of the UDC, Colonel Robert G. Shaver Camp of the SCV and the North East Arkansas Civil War Heritage Trails Committee. There are Confederate flags on display and a Civil War–era cannon, and plans include raising funds for a statue in honor of the Southern soldier.

In his book *Legacy of the Civil War*, Robert Penn Warren summed up that legacy when he wrote, "The Civil War is, for the American imagination, the great single event of our history." Shelby Foote, a historian and novelist of the war, said it even more bluntly when he remarked on the Ken Burns Civil War television documentary: "And it is very necessary, if you're going to understand the American character in the twentieth century, to learn about this enormous catastrophe of the nineteenth century. It was the crossroads of our being, and it was a hell of a crossroads."[107]

Flag display on Beaver Lake. *Courtesy of W. Stuart Towns.*

The celebrations of Memorial Day, the dedications and all the fundraising work of creating monuments to the Confederate soldier and the women standing in support back home and the countless reunions of veterans who met with their comrades to remember the "wah" all helped to create the heritage and tradition of this "great single event"—this "hell of a crossroads." Our nation has not fully settled the debates of the war, and many southerners still expect to be allowed and encouraged to honor their ancestors who fought over those debates.

There have been countless controversies and heated arguments by laymen and historians over strategy, tactics, a particular general's action or lack thereof in a particular battle, the causes of the war and the reasons why the North won and the South lost. But there was essentially no debate among white southerners over the courage, honor and heroism of those who fought and died on both sides and the women who supported them and, after the war's end, honored them with these important ceremonial events.

Let us use the sesquicentennial as a time to get acquainted with the public narrative of the war in Arkansas through these monuments and commemorative events around the state, learn more about our Civil War across our state and region, listen to the stories of all the people touched by the war and, finally, achieve a true national reconciliation.

APPENDIX

SESQUICENTENNIAL HISTORICAL MARKERS COMPLETED

No. 1: The Arsenal Crisis, Little Rock, Pulaski County

No. 2: DeValls Bluff in the Civil War, DeValls Bluff, Prairie County

No. 3: Skirmish at Lunenburg, Melbourne vicinity, Izard County

No. 4: Action at Dardanelle (NHC), Dardanelle, Yell County

No. 5: Chalk Bluff in the Civil War (NHC), St. Francis vicinity, Clay County

No. 6: Action at Whitney's Lane, Searcy vicinity, White County

No. 7: Confederate Records Moved to Rondo, Rondo, Miller County

No. 8: Fighting Near Etowah, Etowah, Mississippi County

No. 9: Tate's Bluff in the Civil War, Camden vicinity, Ouachita County

No. 10: Battle of Arkansas Post, Gillett, Arkansas County

No. 11: Skirmish at Osceola, Osceola, Mississippi County

No. 12: Arkansas Peace Society/Raids on Burrowville, Marshall, Searcy County

No. 13: Skirmish at Tomahawk, St. Joe, Searcy County

No. 14: Batesville in the Civil War, Batesville, Independence County

No. 15: Confederate and Union Occupation of Fort Smith, Fort Smith, Sebastian County

No. 16: Hicks' Station in the Civil War, Lonoke, Lonoke County

No. 17: Berryville in the Civil War, Berryville, Carroll County

No. 18: Civil War Healing, Eureka Springs, Carroll County

No. 19: The Borden House/Legacy of Prairie Grove, Prairie Grove, Washington County

No. 20: Action at Cotton Plant, Cotton Plant, Woodruff County

No. 21: The Civil War in Van Buren County, Clinton, Van Buren County

No. 22: Skirmish at Yocum Creek, Green Forest, Carroll County

No. 23: Mount Holly Cemetery, Mount Holly, Union County

No. 24: General John Porter McCown, Magnolia, Columbia County

No. 25: First Kansas Colored Infantry, Camden, Ouachita County

No. 26: Boone County in the Civil War, Harrison, Boone County

No. 27: Destruction of Saltworks, Bald Knob vicinity, White County

No. 28: Wittsburg in the Civil War, Wittsburg, Cross County

No. 29: Boone-Murphy House, Pine Bluff, Jefferson County

No. 30: Holcomb's Spring in the Civil War, Springdale, Washington County

No. 31: Skirmish at Rolling Prairie, Harrison, Boone County

No. 32: Action at Des Arc Bayou, Gum Springs, White County

No. 33: Mill Burning in Northwest Arkansas, Johnson, Washington County

No. 34: CSS *Pontchartrain*, North Little Rock, Pulaski County

No. 35: Huntersville, North Little Rock, Pulaski County

No. 36: Confederate Fortifications, North Little Rock, Pulaski County

No. 37: General Dandridge McRae, Searcy, White County

No. 38: Naval Combat at West Point, West Point, White County

No. 39: Searcy Landing in the Civil War, Searcy, White County

No. 40: Fourteenth Arkansas Infantry Regiment, Lead Hill, Boone County

No. 41: Memphis to Little Rock Railroad, DeValls Bluff, Prairie County

No. 42: Richmond in the Civil War, Richmond, Little River County

No. 43: Elkins' Ferry/Cornelius Farm, Prescott, Nevada County

No. 44: Moro in the Civil War, Moro, Lee County

No. 45: Prairie D'Ane, Prescott, Nevada County

No. 46: Yellville in the Civil War, Yellville, Marion County

No. 47: Skirmish at Haguewood Prairie, Paris, Logan County

No. 48: Tulip Military Academy, Tulip, Dallas County

No. 49: Cleburne County in the Civil War, Heber Springs, Cleburne County

No. 50: Action at Fitzhugh's Woods, Augusta vicinity, Woodruff County

No. 51: Seven Confederate Generals, Helena–West Helena, Phillips County

No. 52: USCT in Helena, Helena–West Helena, Phillips County

No. 53: Isaac Murphy, Huntsville, Madison County

No. 54: Huntsville Massacre, Huntsville, Madison County

No. 55: Royston Factory Mill/Henry Merrell, Murfreesboro, Pike County

No. 56: Scott County in the Civil War, Waldron, Scott County

No. 57: Fifth Arkansas Infantry Regiment, Paragould, Greene County

No. 58: Judge David Walker, Fayetteville, Washington County

No. 59: Camp Halleck at Osage Springs, Rogers, Benton County

No. 60: Shelling of Jacksonport, Jacksonport, Jackson County

FOR FURTHER READING

The following books are suggested for further reading into the subject of the creation and sustaining of the Lost Cause and the public memory of the Civil War.

Bodnar, John. *Remaking America: Public Memory, Commemoration, and Patriotism in the Twentieth Century*. Princeton, NJ: Princeton University Press, 1992.

Coski, John. *The Confederate Battle Flag: America's Most Embattled Emblem*. Cambridge, MA: Belknap Press of Harvard University Press, 2005.

Cox, Karen. *Dixie's Daughters: The United Daughters of the Confederacy and the Preservation of Confederate Culture*. Gainesville: University Press of Florida, 2003.

Cullen, Jim. *The Civil War in Popular Culture: A Reusable Past*. Washington, D.C.: Smithsonian Institution Press, 1995.

Fahs, Alice, and Joan Waugh. *The Memory of the Civil War in American Culture*. Chapel Hill: University of North Carolina Press, 2004.

Foster, Gaines. *Ghosts of the Confederacy: Defeat, the Lost Cause, and the Emergence of the New South, 1865 to 1913*. New York: Oxford University Press, 1987.

Goldfield, David R. *Still Fighting the Civil War: The American South and Southern History*. Baton Rouge: Louisiana State University Press, 2002.

Johnson, Christina Dunn. *No Holier Spot of Ground: Confederate Monuments & Cemeteries of South Carolina*. Charleston, SC: The History Press, 2009.

Logan, Charles Russell. *Something So Dim It Must Be Holy: Civil War Commemorative Sculpture in Arkansas, 1886–1934*. Little Rock: Arkansas Historic Preservation Program, n.d.

Mayo, James M. *War Memorials as Political Landscape: The American Experience and Beyond*. New York: Praeger, 1988.

McMichael, Kelly. *Sacred Memoires: The Civil War Monument Movement in Texas*. Denton: Texas State Historical Association, 2009.

Neff, John. *Honoring the Civil War Dead: Commemoration and the Problem of Reconciliation*. Lawrence: University Press of Kansas, 2005.

Osterweis, Rollin G. *The Myth of the Lost Cause*. Hamden, CT: Archon Books, 1973.

Poole, W. Scott. *Never Surrender: Confederate Memory and Conservatism in the South Carolina Upcountry*. Athens: University of Georgia Press, 2004.

Prince, K. Michael. *Rally 'Round the Flag, Boys!* Columbia: University of South Carolina Press, 2004.

Towns, W. Stuart. *Enduring Legacy: Rhetoric and Ritual of the Lost Cause*. Tuscaloosa: University of Alabama Press, 2012.

Wilson, Charles Reagan. *Baptized in Blood: The Religion of the Lost Cause, 1865–1920*. Athens: University of Georgia Press, 1980.

NOTES

Introduction

1. Two notable examples are Kelly McMichael, *Sacred Memories: The Civil War Monument Movement in Texas* (Denton: Texas State Historical Association, 2009) and Kristina Dunn Johnson, *No Holier Spot of Ground: Confederate Monuments & Cemeteries of South Carolina* (Charleston, SC: The History Press, 2009).
2. Mark Twain, *Life on the Mississippi* (New York: Penguin Books, 1984), 318–19.
3. Chuck Meyers, "Gettysburg Rehab," *Arkansas Democrat Gazette*, July 7, 2013, 4E.
4. "Remembering Generals Lee and Jackson," *The Civil War Courier*, March 2012, 8.
5. "Texas Rejects Confederate Flag on License Plates," *Denver Post*, November 11, 2011, 17A.
6. Advertisement in *Arkansas Democrat Gazette*, November 15, 2012.

Chapter 1

7. Alfred Moore Waddell, "Memorial Day Address, New Bern, North Carolina, May 9, 1879." *Newbernian*, May 10, 1879. Cited in Towns, *Enduring Legacy*, 22.
8. "Memorial Day, Norfolk, Virginia, June 4, 1891." Undated, unknown newspaper clipping in author's possession.
9. "An Address on Memorial Day, May 20th, 1890, Greenville, S.C., by Rev. Ellison Capers." (Greenville, SC: Daily News Steam Book and Job Presses, 1890).
10. Jefferson Davis, *The Rise and Fall of the Confederate Government* (New York: Thomas

Yoseloff, 1958), frontispiece; Confederated Southern Memorial Associations, *History of Confederated Memorial Associations of the South* (New Orleans: Graham Press, 1904), 330.

11. Mrs. B.A.C. Emerson, "Confederate Monuments by States," *Confederate Veteran* 20, no. 1 (January 1912): 43.

12. Mrs. B.D. M'Leod, "First Confederate Monument," *Confederate Veteran* 13, no. 1 (January, 1905): 11.

13. Towns, *Enduring Legacy*, 31, 35.

14. W. Stuart Towns, "Honoring the Confederacy in Northwest Florida: The Confederate Monument Ritual," *Florida Historical Quarterly* 57, no. 2 (October 1978): 205–12.

15. "Monument to General Robert E. Lee," *Southern Historical Society Papers* 17 (1889): 189.

16. John W. Daniel, "Address of John W. Daniel, LLD." In *Ceremonies Connected with the Inauguration of the Mausoleum and the Unveiling of the Recumbent Figure of General Robert Edward Lee at Washington and Lee University, Lexington, Va., June 28, 1883* (Richmond, VA: West, Johnston & Co., 1883), cited in Towns, *Enduring Legacy*, 105.

17. "Monument to General Robert E. Lee," 188.

18. Michael Kammen, *Mystic Chords of Memory: The Transformation of Tradition in American Culture* (New York: Knopf, 1991), 126.

19. Newspaper clipping in Confederate Monument Subject File in Mississippi State Archives, Jackson, MS.

20. David W. Blight, *Race and Reunion: The Civil War in American Memory* (Cambridge, MA: Belknap Press of Harvard University Press, 2001), 80; *Confederate Veteran* 1, no. 3 (March 1893): 87.

21. "United Confederate Veterans," *Confederate Veteran* 1, no. 1 (January 1893): 11.

22. Cited in Towns, *Enduring Legacy*, 26, note 34.

23. Wallace Evan Davies, *Patriotism on Parade: The Story of Veterans and Hereditary Organizations in America, 1783–1900* (Cambridge, MA: Harvard University Press, 1955), 42.

24. "Orr's Rifles Reunion," *Charleston (SC) News and Courier*, July 24, 1875.

25. Ibid.

26. John Brown Gordon, "The Old South," Augusta, Georgia, April 26, 1887. Reprinted in W. Stuart Towns, *Oratory and Rhetoric in the Nineteenth-Century South: A Rhetoric of Defense* (Westport, CT: Praeger, 1998), 141–48.

CHAPTER 2

27. Most of this material on the Southern Memorial Association comes from these sources unless otherwise indicated: J.C. Walker, "Fayetteville" in James P.

Coffin, comp., "Confederate Cemeteries of Arkansas," *Publications of the Arkansas Historical Association*, Vol. 2 (Little Rock, AR: Democrat Printing and Lithography Co., 1908) 296–97; Rowena McCord Gallaway, compiler and editor, "The Southern Memorial Association of Washington County, Arkansas" (no place, no publisher, 1956); the Southern Memorial Association website; Mrs. Lizzie Pollard, "Southern Memorial Association, Fayetteville, Arkansas," in *History of the Confederated Memorial Associations of the South*; Edward B. Meriwether, "Excerpts from an Address Given at the Confederate Cemetery in Fayetteville, Arkansas on June 2, 1940," *Arkansas Historical Quarterly* 3, no. 4 (Winter 1944): 351–55; and Derek Allen Clements, "Southern Memorial Association of Washington County," *Encyclopedia of Arkansas History & Culture*, http://www.encyclopediaof arkansas.net/encyclopedia/entry-detail.aspx?entryID=4301.

28. Lizzie Pollard, "Southern Memorial Association," *Confederate Veteran* 6, no. 4 (April 1898): 167.

29. Clara B. Eno, *History of Crawford County, Arkansas*, (Van Buren, AR: Press-Argus, no date), 416. The accounts of the following cemeteries are taken from an article in Coffin, *Publications*. Mrs. Fannie Dunham Scott, "Van Buren," 305; Mrs. Margaret T. Rose, "Little Rock," 299–300; Judge A.H. Carrigan "Washington," 301–02; Colonel Jordan E. Cravens, "Clarksville," 302–03; Mrs. J.W. Meek, "Camden," 304; Rev. M. McN. McKay, D.D., "Fort Smith," 306.

30. "Monument at Austin, Ark.," *Confederate Veteran* 15, no. 4 (April 1907): 173; T.J. Young, "Camp Nelson: Lonoke County," in Coffin, *Publications*, 300–01; Mrs. Thomas F. Dodson, "Confederate Monuments and Markers in Arkansas," 187–89, typewritten document produced for Arkansas Division, UDC; News, Notes, and Comments," *Arkansas Historical Quarterly* 41, no. 4 (Winter 1982): 369; Mrs. B.A.C. Emerson, "Austin, Ark.," in *Historic Southern Monuments Representative Memorials of the Heroic Dead of the Southern Confederacy* (New York: Neale Publishing Co, 1911), 46–47.

31. Major Greenfield Quarles, "Helena," Coffin, *Publications*, 298.

32. "Rondo Cemetery," *Arkansas Gazette*, March 1, 1953, from Mrs. James B. Evans scrapbook, in author's possession.

33. Isabel Burthon Anthony, ed., *Garland County, Arkansas: Our History and Heritage* (Hot Springs, AR: Garland County Historical Society, 2009), 136, 211.

34. Reverend James B. Evans, "Memorial Day—May 9, 1954—U.D.C." Speech text in Evans scrapbook, in possession of author.

35. Jacob Worthan, "Camp White Sulphur Springs Confederate Cemetery," *Encyclopedia of Arkansas History & Culture*, http://www.encyclopediaofarkansas.net/ encyclopedia/entry-detail.aspx?entryID=7322.

36. "Memorial Decoration Day," *Lonoke Democrat*, May 1912.

CHAPTER 3

37. "Confederate Monuments by States," 43.

38. The information regarding the Batesville Monument was taken from the website of the Arkansas Historic Preservation Program; *Confederate Veteran* 15, no. 3 (March 1907): 106; and Dodson, "Confederate Monuments," 7–11.

39. This description of the Jacksonport monument comes largely from the website of the Arkansas Historic Preservation Program; *Confederate Veteran* 23, no. 2 (February 1915): 88; ibid. 30, no. 2 (February 1922): 48; ibid. 33, no. 4 (April 1925): 149; Dodson, "Confederate Monuments," 191–211; Clark Reames, "History of Jacksonport," *Stream of History* 21, no. 3 (September 1964): 18–22; William E. Bevens, *Reminiscences of a Private*, ed. Daniel E. Sutherland (Fayetteville: University of Arkansas Press, 1992), xv; "Dedication of Jacksonport State Park," *Independence County Chronicle* 6, no. 4 (July 1965): 6; and Jacksonport State Park Brochure.

40. This account of the Searcy monument is from *White County Heritage* (publication of the White County Historical Association) 3, no. 2: 21; Raymond Lee Muncy, *Searcy, Arkansas: A Frontier Town Grows Up With America* (Searcy, AR: Harding Press, 1976), 184–86.

41. W.E. Orr, *That's Judsonia: An Informal History of a Small Town in Arkansas* (Judsonia, AR: White County Printing Co., 1957).

42. The descriptions of these Mississippi County boulder monuments are from Dodson, "Confederate Monuments," 19–21, 213–15.

43. Ibid., 53.

44. Ibid., 55–57.

45. Ibid., 299. Thanks also to Danny Honnoll, camp commander of the Robert G. Shaver Camp 1655, Sons of Confederate Veterans, who told me where the stone marker could be found.

46. Dodson, "Confederate Monuments," 49–51.

47. *Lee County Courier*, "The Confederate Monument," 21, no. 48, November 19, 1910; *Lee County Courier*, "Lee Statue Unveiled," 21, no. 50, December 10, 1910; Lee County Sesquicentennial Committee, *History of Lee County, Arkansas* (Dallas, TX: Curtis Media Corporation, 1987), 86–87; Dodson, "Confederate Monuments," 175–81.

48. This account of the Helena monuments is taken largely from the following sources: Dale P. Kirkman, "A Brief History of Maple Hill Cemetery," *Phillips County Historical Quarterly* 3, no. 1 (September 1964): 21–27; George E.N. de Man, *Helena: The Ridge, the River, the Romance*, (n.p.: Pioneer Press, 1978), 77–78; Mrs. Paralee Haskell, "Helena," *Confederate Veteran* 1, no. 1 (January 1893): 8; *Harrison*

(AR) Times, June 12, 1886; and Dodson, "Confederate Monuments," 85–89. The reference to Helena as the "leading Confederate Monument city" was in "Maj.-Gen. John J. Horner, Helena, Ark.," *Confederate Veteran* 6, no. 7 (July 1898): 334.

49. George K. Cracraft, "The Chicot County Soldier from 1861 to 1865 and Our Bounden Duty to Him," in Sheila Farrell Brannon, compiler and editor, *A Tribute to Chicot County, Arkansas*, Vol. 1 (2000), 21–25. The other materials of the Lake Village monument are from ibid., 61; Don R. Simons, *In Their Words: A Chronology of the Civil War in Chicot County, Arkansas and Adjacent Waters of the Mississippi River* (Sulphur, LA: Wise Publications, 1999), 169–70; Dodson, "Confederate Monuments," 113–15.

50. Dodson, "Confederate Monuments," 183.

51. Rusty Logan, "Star City Confederate Monument" in Mark K. Christ and Cathryn H. Slater, eds., *Sentinels of History: Reflections of Arkansas Properties on the National Register of Historic Places* (Fayetteville: University of Arkansas Press, 2000), 106–11; Dobson, "Confederate Monuments," 291.

52. "St. Charles Battle Monument, St. Charles, Arkansas County," website of Arkansas Historic Preservation Program; J.M. Henderson Jr., *Brief Stories of St. Charles in Romance and Tragedy* (Dewitt, AR: J.M. Henderson, n.d.), 4–7; Dodson, "Confederate Monuments," 281; Anna Nash Yarbrough, "Along the Highways and Byways," *Arkansas Gazette*, January 18, 1952, clipping in Mrs. James B. Evans scrapbook in author's possession.

53. Dodson, "Confederate Monuments," 107–11.

54. Ibid., 227–31.

55. Jacob Worthan, "Camp White Sulphur Springs Confederate Cemetery," *Encyclopedia of Arkansas History & Culture*, http://www.encyclopediaofarkansas.net/encyclopedia/entry-detail.aspx?entryID=7322; James W. Leslie, "The Mystery of the Sulphur Springs Cemetery," *Jefferson County Historical Quarterly* 8, no. 4, 46–47; Dodson, "Confederate Monuments," 277–79; "Camp White Sulphur Springs Confederate Cemetery, Sulphur Springs, Jefferson County," website of Arkansas Historic Preservation Program.

56. "Monument at Camden, Ark." *Confederate Veteran* 2, no. 7 (July 1894): 216; Dodson, "Confederate Monuments," 25–27; "National Register Adds Confederate Graveyard," *Ouachita County Historical Quarterly* 28, no. 3 (Spring 1997): 11.

57. "Work of the Daughters at Camden, Ark." *Confederate Veteran* 13, no. 9 (September 1905): 406–07.

58. "Monument Nominated," *Ouachita County Historical Quarterly* 27, no. 2 (Winter 1995): 3; Dodson, "Confederate Monuments," 29–33.

59. Dodson, "Confederate Monuments," 233–37; "National Parks, Monuments, and Landmarks," *Ouachita County Historical Quarterly* 17, no.1 (September 1985): 20.

60. Dodson, "Confederate Monuments," 311; website of Arkansas Historic Preservation Program.

61. D.W. Thomas, "El Dorado, Ark." In *Historic Southern Monuments: Representative Memorials of the Heroic Dead of the Southern Confederacy*. Compiled by B.A.C. Emerson), 53–55; Dodson, "Confederate Monuments," 63–67; "Drinking Fountain at El Dorado, Ark." *Confederate Veteran* 18, no. 4 (April 1910): 205.

62. Isabel Burton Anthony, ed., *Garland County, Arkansas: Our History and Heritage* (Hot Springs, AR: Garland County Historical Society and Melting Pot Genealogical Society, 2009), 136–37, 211; "The Confederate Lot in Hollywood Cemetery," *Record*, Vol. 1 (January 1962), 6–9; ibid., Vol. 5 (September 1964), 40–41; *Hot Springs Sentinel-Record*, "Confederate Park Monument Will Be Unveiled Saturday," June 2, 1934; ibid., "Monument to Confederates Unveiled Here," June 3, 1934; Dodson, "Confederate Monuments," 95; *Hot Springs Sentinel-Record*, "Confederate Park Takes on New Look," January 13, 2002.

63. *Southern Standard*, "A Gala Day for the U.D.C.," June 1, 1911; ibid., "To the Descendants of the Men of '61," June 15, 1911. The account of the problem of paying for the monument came from Allen Syler, "The Confederate Monument Clark County Courthouse Square, The Planning, Erecting and Payment as Recorded in the Southern Standard Newspaper, Arkadelphia, Arkansas," *Clark County Historical Journal*, (Fall 1982): 70–91; *Arkansas Democrat-Gazette*, "Soldier Whole Again, Reclaims Post," August 13, 2002, 1B. Trammell statement cited in Towns, *Enduring Legacy*, 143.

64. Miss Ruby E. Livingston, "Confederate Mothers' Park," *Confederate Veteran* 31, no. 11 (November 1923): 435; Dodson, "Confederate Monuments," 271–75; "Confederate Park on Historic Register," *Pope County Historical Association Quarterly* 30, no. 2 (June 1996): 28.

65. "Hundreds Witness the Impressive Ceremony of U.D.C. Unveiling," in *Bits and Pieces: Links That Bind Yell County, Arkansas*, Vol. 1, compiled by Mary Vinson Humphrey and Doyle Traxler, (N.p., 1980), 2–3; Dodson, "Confederate Monuments," 61.

66. "Clarksville Confederate Monument, Clarksville, Johnson County," Arkansas Historic Preservation Program, http://www.arkansaspreservation.com/historic-properties/_search_nomination_popup.aspx?id=1612; Dodson, "Confederate Monuments," 37; Colonel Jordan E. Gravens, "Clarksville," *Publications of the Arkansas Historical Association* 2 (1908): 302–03.

67. Personal observation. No records have been located concerning this monument.

68. Dodson, "Confederate Monuments, 35.

69. "Fort Smith Monuments," *Confederate Veteran* 6, no. 7 (July 1898): 324; "Monument at Fort Smith, Ark.," *Confederate Veteran* 12, no. 1 (January 1904): 18;

"Fort Smith Confederate Monument, Fort Smith, Sebastian County," *Arkansas Historic Preservation Program*, http://www.arkansaspreservation.com/historic-properties/_search_nomination_popup.aspx?id=539; "Fort Smith," in Emerson, *Historic Southern Monuments*, 56–58; Dodson, "Confederate Monuments," 81–83.

70. The information regarding these last three monuments was found on www.Arkansasties.com.

71. "Monument at Van Buren, Ark.," *Confederate Veteran* 7, no. 4 (April 1899): 155; "Miss Fannie M. Scott," *Confederate Veteran* 9, no. 6 (June 1901): 274; Margaret Wood, "Van Buren, Ark.," in Emerson, *Historic Southern Monuments*, 62–65.

72. Rowena McCord Gallaway, comp., ed., "The Southern Memorial Association of Washington County, Arkansas," (no place, no publisher, 1956), 18, 24–26, 40; "Southern Memorial Days," website of Ancestry.com; Walker, "Fayetteville," 296–97; Clements, "Southern Memorial"; Mark K. Christ, "Arkansas Listings in the National Register of Historic Places, Fayetteville National Cemetery and Fayetteville Confederate Cemetery," *Arkansas Historical Quarterly* 71, no. 2 (Summer 2012): 217–21.

73. "News, Notes, and Comments," *Arkansas Historical Quarterly* 39, no. 4 (Winter 1980): 355; "Prairie Grove Battlefield State Park," Arkansas Department of Parks and Tourism brochure; "Prairie Grove Has New Monument," *Flashback* 15, no. 3 (July 1965): 41–42; Dodson, "Confederate Monuments," 241–49.

74. John T. Willett, "Development of Pea Ridge National Military Park," *Arkansas Historical Quarterly* 21, no. 2 (Summer 1962): 166–69; Dodson, "Confederate Monuments," 217–25; J. Dickson Black, *History of Benton County* (Little Rock: International Graphics Industries, 1975), 252–59.

75. Dodson, "Confederate Monuments," 13–17; Emerson, *Historic Southern Monuments*, 48–49; *Confederate Veteran* 16, no. 10 (October 1908): 494; Black, *History of Benton County*, 264–67; Emilee Dehmer, "Confederate Soldier Memorial," unpublished manuscript, Rogers Historical Museum, Rogers, AR.

76. "Monument at Austin, Ark.," *Confederate Veteran* 15, no. 4 (April 1907): 173; Dodson, "Confederate Monuments," 187, 189; "News, Notes, and Comments," *Arkansas Historical Quarterly* 41, no. 4 (Winter 1982): 379; Emerson, *Historical Monuments*, 46–47.

77. "Lonoke Confederate Monument, Lonoke, Lonoke County," Arkansas Historic Preservation Program, http://www.arkansaspreservation.com/historic-properties/_search_nomination_popup.aspx?id=751; Dodson, "Confederate Monuments," 99–101; *Lonoke Democrat*, "Cornerstone of Monument Laid," June 23, 1910.

78. Dodson, "Confederate Monuments," 39–41.

79. Maranda Leeper, "Little Rock National Cemetery," *Encyclopedia of Arkansas History and Culture*, http://www.encyclopediaofarkansas.net/encyclopedia/entry-

detail.aspx?entryID=6968; Dodson, "Confederate Monuments," 131–35; "Little Rock National Cemetery, Little Rock, Arkansas," website of the National Park Service; "National Cemetery Administration Little Rock National Cemetery," website of U.S. Department of Veterans Affairs.

80. The material on the Dodd marker is from Dodson, "Confederate Monuments," 151, and the reference to the Capital Guards monument is from ibid., 127.

81. Mark Waller, "Re-enactors, McMath Honor Teen's Sacrifice," *Arkansas Democrat-Gazette*, January 11, 1998.

82. "U.D.C. Notes," *Confederate Veteran* 31, no. 12 (December 1922): 472; ibid., 32, no. 1 (January 1923): 6; Dodson, "Confederate Monuments," 145.

83. Dodson, "Confederate Monuments," 149.

84. Ibid., 141.

85. James Reed Eison, "A Radiance That Will Illuminate the Name," *Pulaski County Historical Review* 38, no. 1 (Spring 1990): 16–21.

86. Dodson, "Confederate Monuments," 161.

87. Zachary Elledge, "Monument to Confederate Women," *Encyclopedia of Arkansas History & Culture*, http://www.encyclopediaofarkansas.net/encyclopedia/entry-detail.aspx?entryID=7592; Franklin Allen Latimer, "Arkansas Listings in the National Register of Historical Places: The Confederate Soldiers Monument and Monument to Confederate Women in Little Rock," *Arkansas Historical Quarterly* 40, no. 3 (Autumn 2001): 305–10; Dodson, "Confederate Monuments," 159.

88. Dodson, "Confederate Monuments," 125; *Confederate Veteran* 5, no. 1 (January 1897): 39; Latimer, "Arkansas Listings," 305–10; Emerson, *Historic Monuments*, 59–61. The most complete rendering of the process of building this monument is in *Confederate Veteran* 13, no. 8 (August 1905): 350–57. It includes the entire speech of Colonel Morgan.

89. Don Montgomery, "Thomas James Churchill (1824–1905)," *Encyclopedia of Arkansas History & Culture*, http://www.encyclopediaofarkansas.net/encyclopedia/entry-etail.aspx?entryID=92; Thomas W. Cutrer, "SCURRY, WILLIAM READ," Handbook of Texas Online, http://www.tshaonline.org/handbook/online/articles/fsc38 (accessed June 13, 2013). Published by the Texas State Historical Association.

CHAPTER 4

90. Ray Hanley, "The Gray Reunion," *Civil War Times Illustrated* (January/February 1992): 42–63; Ray Hanley and Steven G. Hanley, *Remembering Arkansas Confederates and the 1911 Little Rock Veterans Reunion* (Charleston, SC: Arcadia Publishing, 2006);

Michael D. Polston, "Little Rock Did Herself Proud: A History of the 1911 United Confederate Veterans Reunion," *Pulaski County Historical Review* 29, no. 2 (Summer 1981): 22–32; James D. Russell, "The Gray Parade: Little Rock Hosts the Twenty-first National United Confederate Veterans Reunion," *Pulaski County Historical Review* 59, no. 1 (Spring 2011): 33–42. The previous sources tell in great detail the story of the 1911 reunion. My other sources on this event were "Official About Little Rock Reunion," *Confederate Veteran* 19, no. 6 (June 1911): 275–80 and *Southern Standard (Arkadelphia, AR)*, "The Confederate Reunion," May 25, 1911.

91. This account of the 1928 reunion was drawn largely from various issues of the official magazine of the UCV, *Confederate Veteran*: "The Reunion in 1928," *Confederate Veteran* 35, no. 5 (May 1927): 166; "Next Reunion in Little Rock," ibid. 35, no. 6 (June 1927): 195; "The 1928 Reunion," ibid. 35, no. 8 (August 1927): 314; "Getting Ready for the Reunion," and "Committees for Little Rock Reunion," ibid. 35, no. 11 (November 1927): 404, 436; "Little Rock 'The City of Roses,'" ibid. 36, no. 5 (May 1928): 165; "The Reunion in Little Rock," ibid. 36, no. 6 (June 1928): 204–08. Also, Hanley and Hanley, *Remembering Arkansas Confederates*, 113–16.

92. *Herald-Democrat*, "Memorial Day Program," May 13, 1920, 1.

93. Raymond Lee Muncy, *Searcy, Arkansas: A Frontier Town Grows Up with America* (Searcy, AR: Harding Press, 1976), 183–84.

94. James Logan Morgan, "Early History of the Tom Hindman Camp No. 318 United Confederate Veterans," *Stream of History* (Jackson County Historical Society) 16, no. 4 (October 1978): 27–31.

95. Robert R. Logan, "First Confederate Reunion in Washington County," *Flashback* (Washington County Historical Society) 12, no. 4 (December 1962): 15–16.

96. "The Ex-Confederate Reunion at Gravel Hill," *Pope County Historical Association Quarterly* 18, no. 2 (December 1983): 72–73.

97. *Forrest City Times*, September 19, 1902; ibid., August 16, 1907.

98. *Lonoke Weekly Democrat*, August 30, 1906. From the Lonoke Museum.

99. "Reunion at Bentonville, Arkansas," *Confederate Veteran* 1, no. 11 (November 1893): 347.

CHAPTER 5

100. Information brochure, "Arkansas Civil War Sesquicentennial Commission."

101. Program of Civil War Marker Dedication Ceremony Camp Ground United Methodist Church, September 7, 2013, 10:00 a.m., personal copy; W. Danny Honnoll, "Speech at Dedication Ceremony," personal copy received from Honnoll.

102. Most of this information about the Arkansas Civil War Sesquicentennial Commission's programs and activities are taken from a presentation made by Mark Christ of the Arkansas Historic Preservation Program at the August 2013 meeting of the St. Francis County Historical Society and from *Arkansas Democrat-Gazette*, "Civil War Grants Go to Four Projects," June 20, 2013, 3B.

103. Information on the Helena–West Helena campaign to create a heritage tourism destination came from several sources, including the author's several personal visits to the city to speak with persons involved in the effort, such as Ron Kelley of the Delta Cultural Center, and to observe some of the reenactments and memorial services held in 2012 and 2013. Chris Herrington, "Rising on the River," *Arkansas Democrat-Gazette*, March 31, 2013, 1H; "Helena Event Will Recall 1863 Battle," *Arkansas Civil War Heritage Trail* 21, no. 1 (Spring 2013): 1; "General Cleburne Honored," *Helena World*, March 12, 2013, 1; Program of the "28th Annual Sons of Confederate Veterans Cleburne Memorial Service," March 16, 2013, Confederate Cemetery, Maple Hill Cemetery, Helena, Arkansas.

104. Jack Schnedler, "A Sesquicentennial Summer," *Arkansas Democrat-Gazette*, July 2, 2013, 1E.

105. "126th Old Soldiers Reunion Parade to be Held—Saturday, August 3, 2013," News Release, American Legion Department of Arkansas. For an account of this event in 1914, see *Confederate Veteran* 22, no. 10 (October 1914): 476.

106. Jan Sisk Lawrence, "Area Gears Up for Reunion of the Blue and Grey," www.areawidenews.com/story/1411640.html.

107. Warren and Foote quotations cited in Towns, *Enduring Legacy*, 144, 145.

INDEX

ABOUT THE AUTHOR

W. Stuart Towns, PhD, has spent more than forty years following his passion for southern history. During his educational pursuits in undergraduate and graduate studies, he developed a love for public speaking and the impact words have had on history, especially the history of the American South.

Towns attended the University of Arkansas on a track and cross-country scholarship, where he received his BA degree in 1961. He continued his education at the University of Florida, where he received his MA in 1962 and his PhD in 1972. During his career, he served as chair of the Communication Departments at the University of West Florida, Appalachian State University and Southeast Missouri State University. He retired in 2011.

Dr. Towns had a parallel second career in the U.S. Army, which began when he enrolled in ROTC at the University of Arkansas. While on active duty after graduation, he earned a spot on the U.S. Modern Pentathlon team and competed in the 1964 Olympic Trials in modern pentathlon, fencing and the marathon. After completing his active-duty tour, he served the rest of his military career in the active army reserves in the civil affairs branch, mostly with the 361st CA Brigade in Pensacola, Florida. He took an opportunity to become a member of the Consulting Faculty Program at the U.S. Army Command and General Staff College at Fort Leavenworth, Kansas, in 1973 and served in that role until 1996. Dr. Towns retired as a colonel in the active reserves in 1996.

Towns has written four other books on southern rhetoric and public address history: *Oratory and Rhetoric in the Nineteenth-Century South: A Rhetoric of Defense* (1998); *Public Address in the Twentieth-Century South: The Evolution of a Region* (1999); *"We Want Our Freedom": Rhetoric of the Civil Rights Movement* (2002); and *Enduring Legacy: Rhetoric and Ritual of the Lost Cause* (2012).

He and his wife live in Forrest City, Arkansas.